"Divining Thoughts"

"Divining Thoughts":
Future Directions in Shakespeare Studies

Edited by

Pete Orford with Michael P Jones, Lizz Ketterer, Joshua McEvilia

Cambridge Scholars Publishing

"Divining Thoughts": Future Directions in Shakespeare Studies.
Edited by Pete Orford with Michael P Jones, Lizz Ketterer, Joshua McEvilia

This book first published 2007 by

Cambridge Scholars Publishing

15 Angerton Gardens, Newcastle, NE5 2JA, UK

British Library Cataloguing in Publication Data
A catalogue record for this book is available from the British Library

ISBN (10): 1-84718-379-4, ISBN (13): 9781847183798

TABLE OF CONTENTS

Part Two: Performance and New Comparisons

FOREWORD

The Britgrad conference, inaugurated in 1999 and run by students for students, takes place annually at the Shakespeare Institute of the University of Birmingham in Stratford-upon-Avon. The Institute, founded in 1951 by Professor Allardyce Nicoll, eminent historian of world drama, has long been recognised as a centre of excellence for study of Shakespeare, of the literature and drama of his time, and of performance history. Remarkably, its earliest Fellows, Professors R. A. Foakes, John Russell Brown, and E.A.J. Honigmann, continue to be active as scholars to the present day; in 2001 they were honoured at a special degree congregation celebrating the Institute's 50th anniversary which also saw the award of honorary doctorates to the actors Harriet Walter and Kenneth Branagh. Successive directors of the Institute have been General Editors of the Penguin, New Cambridge and Oxford editions of Shakespeare, editors of *Shakespeare Survey*, published by Cambridge University Press, and of a number of series of scholarly publications. Over the years members of its faculty have contributed greatly to their discipline, and many of its students have themselves achieved international distinction as scholars and teachers. Numerous dissertations undertaken by Institute students have formed the basis of substantial publications in the form of editions, books, and articles in learned journals, and the Institute has been responsible for the biennial International Shakespeare Conference since 1951.

The Britgrad Conference is an admirable initiative which provides a much-needed opportunity for graduate students not only from British universities but from all over the world to present the results of their research on Shakespeare and other early modern drama and to discuss their work with fellow scholars. The papers printed in the present volume, all emanating from a single conference, in 2006, bear witness to the range of current research in this area and to the high standards of scholarship prevailing. It is good to see discussion of relatively neglected dramatists, such as Richard Brome and Thomas Heywood, alongside studies of their more illustrious contemporaries; good also to see the deployment of new and intellectually demanding critical techniques alongside more traditional scholarly approaches. The essays printed here demonstrate that the future of early modern dramatic scholarship and criticism is in good hands. It is a privilege for me to commend the volume and to congratulate both those who have contributed to it and its compilers.

Stanley Wells
The Shakespeare Centre, August, 2007

PREFACE

PETE ORFORD

It can never be said that there is a lack of criticism on Shakespeare. In fact, new scholars of the bard invariably find themselves in awe of the sheer volume of academics who precede them. The scholars who are idealistic or foolish enough to pursue a postgraduate degree in Shakespeare often face their greatest challenge in the initial stages of choosing their topic, when they must find something new to say, lest, like Shakespeare's sonnet 76, the author writes 'still all one, ever the same...So all my best is dressing old words new,/Spending again what is already spent'.

At least fifty per cent of a doctoral thesis must be original; that is to say, that once the views and criticism of the past has been summarised and discussed, the remaining half of the thesis must offer entirely new thoughts on the subject. When the thesis is to be written on Shakespeare, this presents a problem, for the bard's prevailing popularity has ensured that almost everyone, from the Duke of Marlborough to Daffy Duck, has had an opinion on him. When I first started my PhD at the Shakespeare Institute, Russell Jackson, the director at the time, offered the following encouragement to counteract the originality conundrum: for all that has been said on Shakespeare, it hasn't been said by *you*. Each new scholar brings with them their own unique experience and insight to the plays, unlocking new ideas that can only be seen from a fresh point of view.

And so within the vast body of work which constitutes Shakespearean criticism, each young researcher must find their niche, their own platform from which they can express their individual views, adding their own names to the likes of Johnson, Malone, Schlegel, Kott, Wells and Greenblatt. Of course, the trouble with standing upon the shoulders of giants is that it is a very tall height from which to fall, and postgraduate students contemplating their future success must anticipate the extremes to which their work will be received; will they become the next prodigy, that current scholars wax lyrical about, as Cranmer did about Elizabeth, promising 'Upon this land a thousand, thousand blessings/Which time shall bring to ripeness'(*Henry VIII* 5.4.19-20), or shall they be told, as Hal is by his father, that 'The hope and expectation of thy time/Is ruined, and the soul of every man/Prophetically do forethink thy fall'(*1 Henry IV*, 3.2.36-38)?

Such hopes and fears can only be confirmed by time and hindsight. As a writer's reputation grows, so their work will influence others and thus reinforce their position in contemporary scholarship; to that effect there are numerous critical anthologies which celebrate the work of our predecessors, and confirm their status as key thinkers on Shakespeare. In contrast, what this collection offers for the here and now is a rare moment of foresight into what is going to happen next in Shakespeare studies; rather than celebrate what has been written, it anticipates what is going to be written. The articles collected here are the work of the next generation of Shakespeare students. These are postgraduate academics all in the process of completing doctoral theses and progressing on to the beginning of their careers in Shakespeare studies. These are the scholars of tomorrow, the people who eventually will teach future students, write the books and edit the plays. These are the people to whom today's scholars will entrust the future of Shakespearean criticism.

Each of the contributors was present at the Eighth Annual International Shakespeare Conference for Postgraduates, held at The Shakespeare Institute in Stratford-upon-Avon in the summer of 2006. The conference was host to eighty delegates from around the world, each one pursuing new avenues of Shakespeare studies. The collection here is therefore a representation of a larger body of work, and encapsulates the wide range of current research on Shakespeare, his works and that of his contemporaries. The articles have been divided into two broad sections looking at, in the first part, Texts and Contexts, then in the second part, Performance and New Comparisons. However, the great success of these articles lies in their variety as an indication of the many ways in which Shakespeare criticism may develop. Each of these authors has found their own personal niche within which to develop and strengthen their ideas and skills, which in turn will impact on their impressions of, and approaches to Shakespeare.

Opening the selection is Matteo Pangallo's frank and refreshing account of his own endeavours to edit *The Launching of the Mary,* a play that has thus far been consigned to obscurity. Pangallo highlights the many difficulties in editing this challenging manuscript, whilst raising significant questions regarding the merits of reviving this forgotten drama and the particular insights which these forgotten works can provide to our established view of Shakespearean theatre.

Eleanor Collins' article stems from our growing appreciation of Shakespeare's contemporaries and their achievements, which has been one of the major developments in current Shakespeare criticism. Collins has been building upon this move away from Shakespeare-centric research to explore the significance of Queen Henrietta's Men. Her research into this largely unexplored area raises new light on our conceptions of how playing companies of the era developed and used their repertory. The article explores specifically the interaction of the company with Thomas Heywood, and investigates how Heywood's prologues can inform our view of the contemporary attitudes to the company's repertory, challenging the prevalent notion that we can generalise the taste of an audience at an outdoor and indoor theatre.

Shelly Hsin-Yi Hsieh then investigates the bawdy elements of Shakespeare's plays. While A. C. Bradley and other character critics have previously explored the many facets of the great tragic characters and princes in Shakespeare, the bard's lower characters have been largely overlooked. Hsieh redresses this through a methodical and comprehensive appraisal of the bawdy characters of the Renaissance stage, analysing the significance of their portrayal, ethics and resolution within the context of contemporary society to provide the reader with an appreciation of the Elizabethan attitude to crime and sexual offences.

Hsieh's exploration of Shakespeare's drama in the context of contemporary culture is complemented by Dong-Ha Seo's succeeding article on the military culture and its impact upon publications in the Elizabethan era. Seo's meticulous research has provided a unique insight into the Elizabethan public's thirst for military books and how the market for these works is much larger than hitherto expected.

The exploration of text and context continues in Audrey Birkett's article on the publication of Richard Brome's *The Antipodes*. Brome has been an undervalued playwright from the era, who is now growing in popularity among scholars. Birkett presents an engaging discussion of *The Antipodes* in which she is able to draw conclusions on Brome's attitude to the professional sphere he was working in, questioning the author's support of the commercial theatre and highlighting the lack of control which the author had over his play in this era.

Completing the first section of articles, Conny Loder challenges the popular opinion of Richard of Gloucester as a Machiavellian villain, arguing that this is a misconception. She addresses how the view of prior scholars has developed from earlier ideas of Richard amongst Tudor mythology and morality, before then going on to compare Machiavelli's original theory of the prince with the dramatic figure created by

Shakespeare, to reveal how Richard actually undermines and contradicts the convention of critics to pigeonhole him as a stock vice-figure.

The second section opens with Brian Schneider's article on the role of women in the audience of a Renaissance theatre. Schneider's article explores the effect which this growing audience had upon the drama being presented to them. Schneider's innovative research into this area presents a startling conclusion which challenges our common conception of the Elizabethan theatre's attitude to women, and suggests a precedent for the subsequent development of female actors once the theatres reopened.

The subsequent article jumps from its predecessor's new insight into original performances, to a speculation on how modern performances are trying to emulate those of the past. Kelly Jones' work focuses upon the recent attempts to recreate an 'authentic' Shakespearean production at the Globe Theatre in London. Jones explores the theatre's joint function as historical reconstruction and contemporary acting space, exposing the artificiality inherent in the Globe's ambitions to present a theatrical experience identical to that of Shakespeare's time.

Kristine Johansan offers an engaging comparative study by employing Shakespeare's *Titus Andronicus* to draw new insights into Percy Shelley's *The Cenci*, whilst also using the latter to suggest new ways of approaching Shakespeare. By contrasting the two rape victims, Lavinia and Beatrice, Johansan challenges the concept of a raped woman as a victim by applying both modern sensibilities and the work of Mary Wollstonecraft. She reviews the treatment of the two women in their respective plays and the resulting significance that this has upon feminine attitudes.

The penultimate article of the collection, by Will McKenzie, addresses the sonnets, so often neglected in favour of Shakespeare's dramatic works, and re-assesses them as works of modernity. McKenzie builds upon the groundbreaking work of Joel Fineman, and develops his appreciation of modernity in the sonnets by exploring how narcissism influences and shapes these poems.

The concluding article by Miles Gregory reflects upon the remarkable change in fortune which *Cymbeline* has enjoyed in the past twenty years, from a once-neglected play to one which is being staged more now than ever before. Taking the unique perspective of Thomas Kuhn's theory of paradigm shift in science, Gregory applies the theory to *Cymbeline* to explore how the apparent incoherence and instability of the text, which once deterred earlier critics from the play, is now being embraced in the post-modern community to champion this play. It is a fitting close to the collection to reflect upon how a paradigm shift can affect all subsequent thinking on the subject, for it is precisely such an occurrence that may occur within the next generation of Shakespeare scholarship. Just as new historicism has dramatically affected the way in which we approach Shakespeare's plays over the last twenty to thirty years, so too may another major reconsideration be imminent that questions and challenges our current thoughts on the bard.

As I said at the beginning, there is no shortage of criticism on Shakespeare. His work continues to be an important part of our heritage, so the vast amount of writing about him will persevere and grow. Though the presence of Shakespeare in English studies remains a constant, the opinions and approaches we employ are ever-shifting, making the study of Shakespeare a dynamic, fluid and vibrant atmosphere; just as the scholars of the past have been reinterpreted in different eras, either to be revered and reviled, celebrated or challenged, so too shall our current views become equally contestable in the light of future discoveries and shifts in prevailing attitudes.

Within this environment of ever-changing opinions, new scholars continue to join universal debate, wherein any person reading *Hamlet* for the first time can proudly join age-old arguments with new insights. This places scholars at a disadvantage, for while every academic has the opportunity to engage in discussion with the texts of the past, it is by definition a one-way dialogue; we can address the criticism of our predecessors, but not our successors. What this unique collection offers is a rare opportunity to glimpse around the corner at what is coming next, to foresee the oncoming developments in Shakespeare studies, and allow academics the opportunity to engage with the texts of the future.

Note

All quotations from Shakespeare's works are taken from the Oxford Complete Works, edited by Stanley Wells, Gary Taylor, John Jowett and William Montgomery, unless otherwise stated.

PART ONE:

TEXTS AND CONTEXTS

CHAPTER ONE

SELDOME SEENE:
OBSERVATIONS FROM EDITING
THE LAUNCHING OF THE MARY,
OR THE SEAMAN'S HONEST WIFE

MATTEO PANGALLO

The field of early modern drama is full of fascinating stories that, because they do not centre on the person or works of William Shakespeare, have gone largely untold over the years. Many of these unique narratives can be best explored through the rigours of the editorial process. This essay will explore one of those stories and will offer some observations that have come to light in the process of preparing a modern-spelling edition of the Caroline play *The Launching of the Mary, or the Seaman's Honest Wife*. This particular text is unique in that it is written in English, by an Englishman, for the English stage, but it was not written in London, or England, or even Europe. Nor was it written, perhaps most importantly, by someone attached to the professional theatres, either as sharer, actor, or dramatist. In the process of telling this story, I emphasise how important it is that rising generations of scholars learn to interrogate the primary source evidence available in the few manuscript playbooks that have survived.

These playbooks represent the complex intersection between the literary work of the author (with its accompanying ideas of fixity, closure, and permanence) and the theatrical work of the playhouse (with its own ideas of fluidity, circularity, and open-endedness). If the literary work is read ideally as a final product of a univocal, authoritarian (in the literal sense) process, the playbook document should be seen as a multivocal, polysemous process itself. Without this primary manuscript evidence, all theoretical and dramaturgical analyses would be ultimately groundless, for it is this manuscript evidence that helps the theoretical scholar or the dramaturgical scholar determine what, precisely, the text for study actually is or should, ideally, be. Bowers once made the observation that we know someone better as an adult if we have known them as a child and as they have grown older; the same holds true for the evolution of texts. Though the printed work "may stand rejoicing in finished maturity, we must surely understand it with superior intimacy if we have watched its growth and seen its perfection in the very act of shaping", that is, from its origins as a manuscript. We should have a concern, Bowers goes on, "for the childhood and adolescence, awkward or charming, of the living seed of a writer" (Bowers 1966). The image of the awkward adolescent, in fact, is particularly appropriate for the play in question.

The Launching of the Mary was written in 1632 by the nonprofessional dramatist Walter Mountfort and licensed by Sir Henry Herbert, Master of the Revels, in June 1633. It was never printed, probably never performed, and exists only in Mountfort's holograph manuscript. Being a comparatively dull piece of drama and written by an amateur, the play has, in most studies of early modern English theatre, fallen to the periphery, if not off the map altogether. But there is still much to learn about (and from) this peculiar play.

The action of *Launching of the Mary* is set in east London, around the Blackwall shipyard during the early autumn of 1626, and is centered on the building and launching of the East India Company ship *Mary*. The bulk of the main plot consists of extremely long and dramatically-uncompelling exchanges between the Lord Admiral Hobab and several officers of the East India Company. In these encounters, Hobab presents the officers with popular arguments made against the Company and the officers' attempt to refute them through both lengthy argumentation and conspicuous displays of political rhetoric. These scenes are adapted almost verbatim from the 1621 economic tract *A Discourse of Trade*, written by Thomas Mun, one of the Company's actual officers. Though Mountfort demonstrates a remarkable ability in setting the tract into verse and dialogue, the sheer dullness of the material from which he was working renders this part of the play tedious.

The subplot includes two main threads showing the less affluent side of the east London dockyards, and it is in these two threads – particularly the first – that Mountfort's abilities as a dramatist are most apparent. The subplot as a whole, unlike the main plot, is pointedly critical of the East India Company and actually contradicts a number of the defence arguments from the main plot, lending the play a complexity and sophistication that previous commentators, reluctant perhaps to examine the text in any detail, have largely ignored or denied. In the first part of the subplot, we meet five shipyard workmen named, appropriately, Thomas Treenail, Osmond Oakum, Tarquin Tar, Tacklemouth Tallow, and Simon Sheathing Nail. We join them between shifts as they frequent local taverns, swap bad jokes, get drunk, start fights, encounter loose women, rehearse amateur dramatics, and exchange off-hand offensive comments about the Dutch (many details that seem to come almost directly from Mountfort's own life). The second part of the subplot is the story of three wives of East India Company sailors, whose husbands are on a Company ship and have left them alone in London for two years. The first two women, Isabel Nut and Mary Spark, take advantage of the situation to go bar-hopping, get drunk on sugar-infused wine, gorge themselves on pickled oysters, engage in petty thievery, and seduce young apprentices. The third, however – aptly named Dorotea Constance – stays at home, takes up sewing to support herself, and rebuffs a series of suitors (including a clergyman) using such artful rhetoric in her rejections that she convinces all of them to give up their womanising ways and get married. At least one commentator has observed that Dorotea's argumentative speeches echo the style and language of the Company officers in the main plot, though to better effect and with much more conviction (Christensen 2006). The economic, moral, and sexual plight of husbandless wives left in London would have had a personal resonance for Mountfort, who himself left behind in London a wife and possibly children when he sailed on Company business to Ireland, the Netherlands, and for several years Persia.

It is important, at this point, to say a few words about the author, Walter Mountfort, one of the approximately two-hundred nonprofessional playwrights from this period of whom we have any evidence. Biography is particularly critical when the text that survives is in the highly personal and idiosyncratic form of a holograph manuscript, a document that is at once both flexible and, by definition, authoritative. Such is the case with Mountfort and *Launching of the Mary*; indeed, as will be explained, Mountfort seems to have quite literally left his fingerprints upon the play.

In reconstructing Mountfort's life we have an excellent account of much of his career in the Court Minute Books of the East India Company. Unfortunately, fundamental details such as his birth, education, family-life, marriage, and even death are unknown (though a brief entry in the Probate Acts of the Prerogative Court of Canterbury suggests that he was deceased by at least 1647 and succeeded by a son, Francis, and a daughter, Rebecca). All that we know for certain of the man comes from his employment and from his play – a work that reveals a man well-read in both contemporary and classical writers (borrowing from economic and political tracts, royal genealogies, several classical authors, Cervantes's *Don Quixote*, and a number of other works), who spoke and read Latin and Dutch, was a theatre-goer, and was familiar with rudimentary theatrical jargon and the format of both print and manuscript plays.

We do not know precisely when he began working for the Company, but as early as August 1615 Mountfort was in their employ as an assistant and was praised by his superiors for his "honesty, sufficiency, and civility". He was soon promoted, and by 1618 he was entrusted with the important task of provisioning ships before departure. The year 1621 is the first we begin to see what may have been Mountfort's greatest fault: he was either extremely incompetent in his bookkeeping or he was defrauding the Company. The administrators of the Company decided upon the latter. When he was confronted on the charge of "short accompting" to the impressive sum of thirteen hundred pounds, Mountfort denied the allegations and refused to submit his books for review. It was only with the threat of suspension for his "great slackness" that Mountfort handed them over. There is no indication in the Company records of what happened next, but over the next several years – despite occasionally getting in trouble for speaking "overboldly" and, on one occasion, starting a tavern brawl – the Company continued to employ him in various, oftentimes sensitive capacities, such as delivering diplomatic letters to the English ambassador at The Hague.

In July 1623, following a routine voyage to Ireland, Mountfort ran into further trouble. The Company discovered he was unable to account for seven thousand pounds of hard currency and one thousand pounds worth of pepper and cloves that had been entrusted to him. On 21 November, a report was issued to the Court remarking that Mountfort's records were too poorly kept to be decipherable. The Court decided that until the auditors could be satisfied no further salary or employment would be issued him. In short, he was dismissed from the Company. Undaunted, Mountfort solicited the Court for several years, seeking back-wages and some form of good employment. A few years later things had evidently taken a turn for the worse, for in a petition dated 18 August 1624, he is described as seeking "relief in his poverty and infirmity". Over the next four years Mountfort continued his petitions and in 1628 engaged the assistance of some sympathisers further advanced in the ranks of the Company to solicit on his behalf. The tactic turned out to be effective.

On 9 March 1629, the Company hired Mountfort as lieutenant onboard the ship *Charles*. They sailed from the Downs on 10 April 1629, reaching Persia on 20 January 1630. There, Mountfort took charge of shipping silk between Ispahan and Gombroon and was lauded by the local English merchants for being "honest and well-governed". Two years later, in April 1632, Mountfort joined up with *Blessing*, another, smaller Company ship. *The Blessing* left Gombroon that month and over the course of a year made her way back to London, her hold filled with several hundred tons of precious raw silk bales in sealed containers. It was at this point, during the long voyage home, that Mountfort wrote his play. The possibility that Mountfort intended, at this point, to pursue a professional London playing company to produce the work cannot be determined, but it is clear that the work was meant as a direct reflection of the clerk's own life. The story of the play is in fact structured upon a juxtaposition that is evidently autobiographical: praising in the main plot, while criticizing in the subplot, the Company that had at times advanced Mountfort's career and fortunes while at other times censuring him and suspending his employment. He pays particular attention in the play to the Company's diligence and strictness with their clerks and accountants, as well as the sense of elation at the good fortune in finding employment with them after many fruitless petitions, the scandalous danger in detraction and gossip, and the inexorable sense of managerial surveillance and social stratification that the officers of the Company exercised over their workers and their families.

It is possible, also, to consider the physical manuscript of the play as a chronicle in microcosm of Mountfort's voyage back to London in 1632. The variation of the ink on the folio pages suggests it was written over a long period of time, sometimes perhaps by candle-light in a cabin, but often out upon the deck. There seem to be water stains on some pages and, as the Malone Society editor of the play, J. H. Walter, observed, "[i]t seems possible that one of the inks used was very susceptible to sea air" and had begun to fade even while the document was being written, requiring the author to write over some words in a darker ink at a later date (Walter 1933). Still, for a play written onboard a ship at sea it is surprising that there are no portrayals of life at sea in the drama. Even the scene of the launching of the ship sets the principal action off-stage in the tiring house. It might also seem peculiar that a play written by a clerk in the East India Company, after having been in India and Persia for several years and at the time of writing still on the sea, is not set in the exotic lands of the east and is not actually a travel drama at all. But perhaps his decision to write what is, in essence, a domestic city comedy of London represents Mountfort's own nostalgic memories of the community from which he had been absent for so many years and to which he soon would be returning.

After a year-long voyage fraught with peril and near disasters, *Blessing* finally made her way up the Thames and returned to the Isle of Dogs in

April 1633. It was the end of a long voyage for *The Blessing*, but the beginning of the end for Mountfort's career, for when the bales of silk for which he was responsible were disembarked from the ship it was discovered that two of the containers held no silk at all. Only stones and dirt. On 22 May the Company launched a formal inquisition.

The inquiry dragged on for two years, with testimony drawn from factors in Persia, investigators searching the houses of Company employees in London, and the Court repeatedly dragging Mountfort and other crew members and officers from *Blessing* before them, threatening torture in Star Chamber if the Company's property was not recovered. It was a bitter affair, with individuals – including Mountfort – offering names to be added to the Company's "Black Book". In an effort to exonerate themselves, men who were formerly shipmates and friends turned on one another, and in the end a number were fined and even more were fired. The whole business drove Mountfort back into illness (or at least into professional concealment), for on several occasions his wife was made to appear on his behalf before the Court. Nonetheless, there seems good evidence that Mountfort's name ended up in the clear. The Court never found him guilty and even ended up paying him his due wages, along with other damages. G. E. Bentley's comment that Mountfort was "probably a dishonest man" due to his "shady career" (Bentley 1967) seems unfairly hostile and, as there is no evidence he was ever convicted on the charges, flatly untrue. What became of the contentious clerk is unknown – though his career as a playwright apparently began and ended with *The Launching of the Mary*.

The biography of the playwright leads into the next topic for consideration when confronting the task of editing a play that exists only in holograph copy: an assessment of the manuscript itself, its important features, its provenance, and what it has to tell us about the history of its creation, revision, and transmission. A manuscript playbook, by definition, has inscribed upon it the markings that reveal the process of circulation and production in the theatre industry of the day; it is this system of marking and revising that most obviously confronts the manuscript editor and presents the most fundamental challenges. What will be defined as the preferred version to be represented in the modern edition? What, to use W. W. Greg's term, is to be the editor's copy-text? The original authorial draft? The author's *currente calamo* corrections? The author's later creative changes? Deletions or revisions required by the Master of the Revels? Dramaturgical requirements inserted, removed, or rewritten by the bookkeeper depending on the exigencies of the venue, actors, or audience? Creative changes or additions made by a collaborator, or even a later reviser? All of these layers? Some of them? If not all, which will be privileged, and why? If we accept that the play existed not as one singular work with many versions but, rather, multiple consecutive autonomous works (in Tanselle's definition of the word), the manuscript editor must deal with the difficulty of simultaneously giving voice to a multitude of speakers that have become, as James Thorpe puts it, "entangled". It becomes clear immediately that these plays (even those that survive only in print) are not single notes that sound once in a linear progression but, rather, full, sonorous chords that repeat, diminish, and sometimes double back in a network of sound.

Thus, the manuscript editor must be grounded in the physical conditions of the text. By examining features such as inks, hands, paper, and stylistic idiosyncrasies, we can peel apart the various layers of composition and revision in order to see both the playwright and the playhouse (and its agents, whether creative, censorial, or dramaturgical) at work. Doing so shows that the plays of this period underwent a transmission process that allowed for substantive, often non-authorial, revisions at almost every stage, thus compelling the writer to, in effect, "collaborate" with all of the conditions that might mitigate his text's ultimate enactment upon the stage. This was certainly complicated by the fact that each of these conditions had its own priorities, not always in accord with those of the playwright or the play. All worked both *upon* and, in a tangible, material sense, *into* the plays of the day and all left their marks upon the surviving manuscripts.

Whereas most editors working from a print copy-text strive to collate, conflate, and emend disparate versions of a work in order to trace one, or usually more, evolutionary lines of textual descent back to a putatively "authoritative" version, it is the responsibility of the editor working from a unique manuscript copy-text to *dissect* the multiple versions within the single body of the work, unraveling them, pulling them apart, and considering them distinct from one another in order to find how they relate to each other and the theatrical process, and to identify the unique, organic evidence incorporated into the material body of the text as a requisite feature of its conditions of composition and revision. The two editorial processes are rigorous and challenging, but each seems to require an approach to the text that is, fundamentally, at odds with the other. If the print editor is a painter, with the text's variant versions as palette and chosen copy-text as canvas, adding swathes of color and lines to create (often in no less an inventive and imaginative way than the author) a singular text, then the manuscript editor must be a sculptor, chipping away at layers of sometimes ossified, sometimes accreted material in an attempt to excavate, or at least suggest, the network of causation between the layers encountered. In this process, the manuscript editor must be able to discern the variant voices that may be encountered and use that evidence to come to a conclusion regarding the text's creation, revision, and transmission. In the case of *Launching of the Mary* there is an ironic abundance *and* deficiency of this evidence. As a manuscript playbook that passed through the hands of an author, a bookkeeper, and the Master of the Revels, it bears important markings tracing its circulation (in a literal sense) through the early modern production process. However, its status as a work by a nonprofessional in the theatre industry – a man closer to the audience than the stage – seems to have relegated it to what the modern editor would call "the slush pile". There is no certain evidence it was performed and for centuries it has been neglected by subjective readers and (ostensibly) objective scholars alike.

In preparing a new, modernised edition of the play, it seems most useful for readers and faithful to the original text to re-present the manuscript using a system of symbols and character colours to visually enfold into one text the manuscript's various layers of inscription and revision. This synoptic system, though admittedly highly interventionist, seems preferable to an apparatus such as a parallel text, which, by reducing the text to simply "before" and "after" and omitting anything between, over-simplifies the complex process of transmission and revision, thus manufacturing a nonexistent hierarchical binary of the "author's version" and the "stage's version". Reproducing *all* discernible layers in the manuscript – thus allowing the reader to "unfold" (in Bernice Kliman's terms) the version most suitable for his or her needs – is surely preferable to presenting a falsely "authoritative" text made up of only one arbitrarily privileged layer or some eclectic and partial combination of several; furthermore, it emphasises the potentially destabilizing effect that the play's identity as a *performance* text has upon any assumed notion of an idealised or singular version of the play. In determining how to unravel the text, therefore, one must look to the documentary evidence to attempt to determine the order, cause, and effect of the various versions.

Based on the patterns of the inks and hands in the manuscript, it is clear that the play underwent an almost circular revision cycle from author to bookkeeper to Master of the Revels, then back to the author and finally the bookkeeper again (or, in some places, apparently the author and bookkeeper simultaneously). During the initial composition process onboard *Blessing* in 1632, Mountfort made various *currente calamo* revisions, some literary, some mechanical. These revisions, ideas that were reconsidered or rejected in the process of composition, show Mountfort's

creative process at work. There is also evidence that Mountfort was
copying some of the pages from an earlier draft that has since been lost;
this would explain why the last lines on several pages appear
unnecessarily cramped onto the bottom of the sheet (implying that the
sheet was then inserted in place of a previously removed page and had to
match up with the start of the next page). Other evidence can be distilled
from the manuscript to provide clues as to the system used in drafting the
play; for example, missing or mislined speech prefixes on some pages
could imply that the playwright wrote out a full page of dialogue and
afterwards went back to add in the necessary speakers' names (though
this, too, may be evidence that Mountfort was working from previously
drafted pages that he may have been revising as he copied them out).

The play thus drafted – part foul paper and part fair copy – was given
to a professional playing company (most likely the second Prince Charles'
Company[1]) in the spring of 1633. The company, making only a few very
small changes to the script at this point, submitted it to Herbert for his
license. Herbert made a number of substantial deletions, marking for
removal references to diplomatically sensitive trade and foreign relations
issues, politically and religiously offensive matter, and many (but,
importantly, not all) oaths and curses.

The marked-up copy was given back to Mountfort, who—despite
being in the midst of the silk bale fiasco—made a number of revisions to
work around Herbert's deletions. This occasioned the insertion of two
addition-slips over particularly sensitive speeches that had been deleted
and the removal of several entire pages that were subsequently replaced by
new pages with new scenes on them. No effort was made to work around
smaller deletions, such as the removal of oaths and curses. Interestingly,
Mountfort also seems to have made a few theatrical revisions at this point;
they are minor, but they inarguably imply the integral role the dramatist
(even a nonprofessional such as Mountfort) played in the process of
modifying his text for the exigencies of the stage. In fact, Mountfort at one
point in the middle of a stage direction, rather than providing a description

---

[1] Bentley (1967) claims that the bookkeeper's addition of interactive music prove
the play was in the hands of one of the private playhouse companies, but it is
generally accepted that, certainly by 1633, the practice of interact music had made
its way into the outdoor theatres as well (Gurr 1994). The play contains conflicting
evidence throughout in regards to the kind of theatrical space for which it was
written, adding to the probability (discussed below) that it was never performed.
The case for all of the British Library Egerton manuscript plays (of which
Launching of the Mary is one) belonging to the second Prince Charles Company
was made originally and most cogently by Frederick Boas.

of what is to happen, merely writes that all "shall be showed before the day of action" (that is, the day of the performance). In other words, he expected to be involved with the rehearsal process, in a role almost akin to that of a modern director's, to provide the actors with the appropriate blocking and serve as mediator to fill in the dramaturgical lacunae of the text itself. In effect, the playwright wrote himself into the very body of the text.

There is another unusual, perhaps unique feature in this manuscript that seems to date from this round of revisions and that also represents the author "writing" himself into his work: literal fingerprints. On several pages it appears that Mountfort has accidentally placed his thumb into blots of ink and left his thumbprints on the paper (on one page, there are two prints squarely opposite each other in the margins, indicating precisely how he held the leaf). Walter Benjamin's metaphorical fingerprints of the storyteller made tangibly real, they are a reminder of the materiality of the text and the physicality of the cultural mechanisms that produced it and left their marks upon it, manifested most obviously in the people that worked upon it.

Finally, the manuscript was partially marked up by the bookkeeper of a professional London playing company. This hand went through the manuscript—apparently immediately after Mountfort's final revisions, though at one point possibly simultaneously with him—and added cues for music between the acts, cut several long, undramatic speeches, and added bits of dialogue to patch up around the cuts. Most drastically, the bookkeeper cut almost the entirety of the revised pages that Mountfort had inserted—removing, in the process, two and a half scenes.

The question of the bookkeeper's hand in the play brings up an important final point: the theatrical evidence in the manuscript that tells us about production practices and materials of the Caroline stage. Or, to be more precise, what it *fails* to tell us. *The Launching of the Mary* has been classified by every previous commentator as one of the eighteen (by Long's count) manuscript playbooks that survive from this period. Their assumption has been that the presence of Herbert's license and the few cues for music added by the bookkeeper are sufficient evidence of the play's eventual performance. But a closer examination of the internal and external evidence, or, more precisely, the general *lack* of sufficient evidence, suggests that this is highly tenuous.

The argument made by commentators such as Margot Heinemann (1980) and John Henry Walter (1933) is that the play was possibly commissioned for a private command performance by the East India Company (though given Mountfort's less than exemplary relationship with the Company at this time, combined with the overtly critical material in the subplot, this is difficult to believe). This imagines a situation in which the Company put up the funds for the play to go forward as a kind of promotion or propaganda, or, to be blunt, a five-act advertisement. There are two objections to this theory. First, the fact that Herbert's license is on the play is evidence that it was to be performed *publicly*; there is no evidence that the Master of the Revels ever licensed a play to be performed for a private audience, only for the public playhouses. The second objection is based on what we know about the early East India Company. The Company at this time was scrupulous in keeping records of all its activities, especially those that involved any expenditure of precious capital. The Court Minute Book, the Calendar of State Papers Colonial, and the Company Letter Books are filled with detailed records of financial transactions large and small, including efforts to promote the company, such as funding the publication of tracts and books or, in 1623, the attempt to sponsor a public play (a project that eventually fell through). The absence of any mention of Mountfort's play in all these sources strongly suggests that such an event did not occur, or, at the very least, renders it impossible to speculate so certainly that it did.

The second option, the one assumed as fact by most previous commentators, is that the play was performed at a public theatre in London (Bentley 1967, Boas 1923, Greg 1931, Heller 1998, King 1971). It is undeniable that the play was in the hands of a professional company, probably the second Prince Charles Company. But there is insufficient dramaturgical evidence in the manuscript itself to suggest that it is actually a finished playbook used on the stage at any point later in the production process than what might be conjectured as an "exploratory" rehearsal or reading. We know from the evidence in other playbooks what types of alterations bookkeepers and actors needed to institute to make a script usable on the stage. And yet, in *The Launching of the Mary*, in the places we would expect to see the hand of the bookkeeper sorting things out, the manuscript is eloquently silent. It has been established by Paul Werstine and other textual scholars that no extant playbook from the period conforms precisely to the ideal form a stage script would assumedly take, but this manuscript is particularly pronounced in its theatrical gaps. We would expect to see the bookkeeper honing down permissive stage directions, adding cues for props (at least twice in the manuscript props instantaneously appear on stage with no warning, cue, or stage direction), removing unnecessary supernumeraries, adding missing speech prefixes, putting in warnings for actors, adjusting contradictory descriptions of the venue (see footnote above), anticipating obvious cuts that the Master of the Revels would make (particularly oaths), and clarifying any of the author's discursive and theatrically useless stage directions. But such changes are absolutely nowhere to be found in the manuscript. The overall lack of such corrections strongly suggests the play was never performed.

It might be argued at this point that the company simply used a different, no longer extant manuscript as the playbook – perhaps in fair copy, removing the censor's cuts and rejected authorial readings. Many commentators support this argument, taking as evidence Herbert's command in his license that he be provided with "a fair copy hereafter". There are, however, two reasons this is unlikely. First, fair copies that were marked up in rehearsal in preparation for conversion into a finished "prompt" copy would bear a reasonable number of theatrically relevant markings from the rehearsal process; *Launching*, as has been mentioned, has far too few. Second, there are at least two stages of revision (from both the author and the bookkeeper) subsequent to the Master of the Revels's deletions and the request, in his license, to be presented with "a fair copy hereafter". If a second, fairer copy was to be made, the addition slips, revisions, and deletions from the bookkeeper would logically have appeared *only* in that second copy and would not have been entered into the first copy, which would have been discarded once the second copy was made. The most likely scenario, then, is that the play was in the possession of a company who, despite seeing it through a series of revisions and possibly a rehearsal, ultimately – perhaps moved to reluctance by its generally undramatic nature – jettisoned the project before it could reach the stage.

In the prologue to his play, Mountfort writes, "The launching of a ship? This modern age/Hath seldom seen such action on a stage./Unseen things seen are most and best approved;/Gold, because rare, is dear and well-beloved". While we might dispute whether this action was – as these lines wishfully relate – ever finally seen upon the stage, the premise that Mountfort offers here holds true for all of the extant manuscript playbook. These texts – seldom seen, rarely studied, almost never performed – deserve our attention, but not simply because they are rare: they provide the most direct evidence of the theatre industry of their day, and they connect us in a tangible way to the lives and stories of the unique individuals who produced this drama. If the present generation of scholars ignores them, disregards what their small but telling details have to teach us, or neglects the practice of manuscript editing in general, we shall do future generations a grave disservice. As Mountfort cautions in his play, "A thing but seldom seen may be forgot".

Works Cited

Adams, Joseph Quincy. "The Authorship of Two Seventeenth-Century Plays", in *Modern Language Notes* (1907): 135-7.

—. ed. *The Dramatic Records of Sir Henry Herbert, Master of the Revels, 1623-1673.* Oxford University Press: Oxford, 1917.

Bawcutt, N. W., ed. *The Control and Censorship of Caroline Drama: The Records of Sir Henry Herbert, Master of the Revels, 1623-1673.* Oxford University Press: Oxford, 1996.

Bentley, Gerald E. *The Jacobean and Caroline Stage.* Oxford: Oxford University Press, 1967.

Boas, Frederick. *Shakespeare and the Universities.* Basil Blackwell: Oxford, 1923.

British Library MS Egerton 1994, folios 317 – 349.

Chaudhuri, K. N. *The English East India Company: The Study of an Early Joint-Stock Company, 1600-1640.* Frank Cass and Company: London, 1965.

Christensen, Ann. "'Absent, weak, or unserviceable': The East India Company and the Domestic Economy in *The Launching of the* Mary, *or The Seaman's Honest Wife*". Unpublished paper; forthcoming in *Global Trade* (University of Houston).

Dessen, Alan and Leslie Thomson. *A Dictionary of Stage Directions in English Drama, 1580-1642.* Cambridge University Press: Cambridge, 1999.

Dutton, Richard. *Licensing, Censorship, and Authorship in Early Modern England.* Palgrave: New York City, 2000.

Farrington, Anthony. *A Biographical Index of East India Company Maritime Service Officers, 1600-1834.* British Library: London, 1999.

—. *A Catalogue of East India Company Ships' Journals and Logs, 1600 – 1834.* British Library: London, 1999.

Fuller, Tony. *East India Company Ships, 1600 to 1833.* Unpublished catalogue; September 2000; British Library, OIR 382.094.

Gabler, Hans Walter. "Textual Studies and Criticism", in *New Directions in Textual Studies* (eds. David Oliphant and Robin Bradford) Harry Ransom Humanities Research Center: Austin, 1990; pp. 151-165.

Greg, W. W. *Dramatic Documents from the Elizabethan Playhouses.* Oxford University Press: Oxford, 1931.

Gurr, Andrew. *The Shakespearian Playing Companies.* Oxford University Press: Oxford, 1996.

—. *The Shakespearean Stage.* Cambridge University Press: Cambridge, 1994.

Heinemann, Margot. *Puritanism and Theatre: Thomas Middleton and opposition drama under the early Stuarts.* Cambridge University Press: Cambridge, 1980.

Heller, Samantha. "Marks and Traces: Crown, Company, and *The Launching of the Mary*". Unpublished paper presented to the Renaissance Society of America Conference (March 1998).

Holland, Peter, and Stephen Orgel, eds. *From Script to Stage in Early Modern England.* For the Huntington Library; Palgrave Macmillan: New York City, 2004.

Ioppolo, Grace. *Revising Shakespeare.* Harvard University Press: Cambridge, Massachusetts, 1991.

King, Thomas J. *Shakespearean Staging, 1599-1642.* Harvard University Press: Cambridge, Massachusetts, 1971.

Kliman, Bernice. *The Enfolded Hamlets: Parallel Texts.* AMS Press: New York City, 2004.

Kusunoki, Akiko. "'Their Testament at Their Apron-strings': The Representation of Puritan Women in Early Seventeenth-Century England", in *Gloriana's Face: Women, Public and Private, in the English Renaissance* (eds. S. P. Cerasano and Marion Wynne-Davies). Harvester Wheatsheaf: Hemel Hempstead, 1992.

Lawson, Philip. *The East India Company: A History.* Longman: London, 1993.

Long, William. "'Precious Few': English Manuscript Playbooks", in *A Companion to Shakespeare* (ed. David Scott Kastan). Blackwell: Oxford, 1999, pp. 414-433.

Maquerlot, Jean-Pierre and Michèle Willems, eds. *Travel and Drama in Shakespeare's Time.* Cambridge University Press: Cambridge, 1996.

Masten, Jeffrey. "Playwrighting: Authorship and Collaboration", in *A New History of Early English Drama* (eds. John Cox and David Scott Kastan). Columbia University Press: New York City, 1997, pp. 357-382.

Mun, Thomas. *A Discourse of Trade, from England unto the East-Indies, Answering to diverse objections which are usually made against the same.* STC 18256; printed by Nicholas Okes for John Pyper: London, 1621.

Pangallo, Matteo. "A New Source for a Speech in *The Launching of the Mary*", in *Notes and Queries.* Vol. 53, No. 4 (December 2006); pp. 528-531.

Proudfoot, Richard. "Dramatic Manuscripts and the Editor", in *Editing Renaissance Dramatic Texts* (ed. Anne Lancashire). Garland: London, 1976; pp.9-38.

Rasmussen, Eric. "The Revision of Scripts", in *A New History of Early English Drama* (eds. John Cox and David Scott Kastan). Columbia University Press: New York City, 1997, pp. 441-460.

Sainsbury, Ethel, ed. *Calendar of State Papers, Colonial Series: East Indies, China, and Persia* (1625-1629 and 1630-1634 vols.). For the Public Records Office; Longman and Company: London, 1884.

Schäfer, Jürgen. "The Orthography of Proper Names in Modern-Spelling Editions of Shakespeare", in *Studies in Bibliography* 23. 1970; p.1-19.

Stern, Tiffany. "'A small-beer health to his second day': Playwrights, Prologues, and First Performances in the Early Modern Theatre", in *Studies in Philology*. Vol. 101, No. 2 (Spring 2004); pp. 172-199.

Sutton, Jean. *Lords of the East: The East India Company and its Ships.* Conway Maritime Press: Greenwich, 1981.

Tanselle, G. Thomas. *A Rationale of Textual Criticism.* Philadelphia: University of Pennsylvania Press, 1989.

—. *Textual Criticism and Scholarly Editing.* For the Bibliographical Society of the University of Virginia; University Press of Virginia: Charlottesville, 1990.

Thorpe, James. *Principles of Textual Criticism.* The Henry E. Huntington Library and Art Gallery: San Marino, 1972.

Tuck, Patrick. *The East India Company, Vol. I.* Routledge: New York, 1998.

Walter, John Henry, ed. *The Launching of the Mary, by Walter Mountfort,* for the Malone Society. Oxford University Press: Oxford, 1933.

Warren, Michael. "The Theatricalisation of Text: Beckett, Jonson, Shakespeare", in *New Directions in Textual Studies* (eds. David Oliphant and Robin Bradford). Harry Ransom Humanities Research Center: Austin, 1990; pp. 39-59.

Wells, Stanley. *Re-Editing Shakespeare for the Modern Reader.* Oxford University Press: Oxford, 1984.

Wells, Stanley and Gary Taylor. *Modernizing Shakespeare's Spelling.* Oxford University Press: Oxford, 1979.

Werstine, Paul. "Plays in Manuscript", in *A New History of Early English Drama* (eds. John Cox and David Scott Kastan). Columbia University Press: New York City, 1997, pp. 481-497.

CHAPTER TWO

THOMAS HEYWOOD AND THE CONSTRUCTION OF TASTE IN THE REPERTORY OF QUEEN HENRIETTA'S MEN

ELEANOR COLLINS

In terms of critical scholarship, Queen Henrietta's Men have occupied an ambiguous status. For many students and scholars working in Shakespearean drama, familiarity with their repertory remains beyond the call of duty. But operating from and performing within the Cockpit (or Phoenix) theatre - one of the "private" hall playhouses of the seventeenth century - they became the closest rivals to the King's Men in the 1630s. Shakespeare-centric readings of Renaissance drama companies have left the importance of Queen Henrietta's Men to theatre history in the dark, despite the implications that the company has for an analysis of competitive repertory strategies in the period. Foundational texts in theatre history tend to classify the company and its repertory according to the key methodological categories of audience and proximity to court, and as a consequence, Queen Henrietta's Men are typically attributed a prestigious, up-market position, playing for audiences that could afford the more expensive admission fee of the indoor theatres. These dual recommendations are linked through an assumption that the company catered to refined and sophisticated audience tastes. In both theatre history and the discourses that permeate prefatory material of the early modern period, these tastes are defined in opposition to those inferred from the dramatic activity of the citizen amphitheatres. Known for their spectacular tear-throat and drum-and-trumpet plays, the amphitheatres provided cheap entertainment for an audience conceptualised as plebeian and culturally negligible. In contrast to constructions of the Cockpit repertory, it is consistently assumed that plays written for the Red Bull amphitheatre were designed to sate the undiscerning appetites of "ignorant asses", and a "Greasie-apron Audience" - spectres that loom out at us from the murky and layered depths of prologues and prefatory material.[1] These audience constructions, compounded by a Restoration recollection of the "meaner sort of people", have been mapped onto plays that have come to represent a dramatic "type" characteristic of citizen fare. G. E. Bentley describes *The Seven Champions of Christendom* as "the sort of spectacular, naïve, and formless piece that one learns to associate with the Red Bull theatre".[2] As Bentley's remark suggests - and perpetuates - the Red Bull's reputation is particularly flagrant. In terms of aesthetic agenda and social standing, it is diametrically opposed to everything that private playhouses - such as the Cockpit - are supposed to be.

So with surprise and reticence theatre historians are forced to recognise the extent to which Queen Henrietta's Men appropriated and exploited Red Bull revivals on the Cockpit stage. The conception of the company as a supplier of plays tailored to the demands of an audience assumed to possess high financial resources and cultural competence is persistently dogged by this inheritance - an inheritance founded less on economic necessity and pragmatism by this time, than on an active repertory stratagem. Revivals remained a core component of the repertory, despite the number of new plays that the Cockpit accumulated. Furthermore, this new fare made active attempts to capitalise upon its relation to revived drama. So this repertory strategy was founded not only upon economic exigency, but also relied upon the *continuity* of taste, across theatre spaces, companies and time. The movement of plays considered to be circumscribed in accordance with the projected mental capacity of its "vulgar" and "plebeian" audience from the realm of "public" to "private" theatrical experience belies any unproblematic distinction between drama "written for" one kind of theatre over another, with implications for the extent to which conditions of reception from an audience determined the repertory management. I believe that the

---

[1] John Webster likens the original auditors of his play to "those ignorant asses (who visiting Stationers shoppes their use is not to inquire for good bookes, but new bookes)" in the note "To the Reader" of *The White Devil,* published in 1612. The title-page attribution is to the Queen's Majesties' Servants (Queen Anna's), who performed at the Red Bull until 1616/7. The prologue to Thomas Dekker's *If It Be Not Good The Devil Is In It,* also published in 1612 and performed "by the Queenes Majesties Servants: At the Red Bull" refers to the "Greasie-apron Audience" (both plays accessed on *Early English Books Online,* http://eebo.chadwyck.com/home, on 8th July 2007).

[2] Bentley, *The Jacobean and Caroline Stage,* IV, p. 712.

disconnect between these narratives of the Cockpit and the provenance of its repertory—as a supplier of refined, mannered plays that nevertheless exploited "thumping" Red Bull plays— is accountable for the hesitation of theatre historians to examine the repertory of Queen Henrietta's Men in its entirety. From this realisation, I argue that the resistance of this repertory to such reductive categorisation has further implications for the restructuring of current theatre history narratives.

One of the key underpins from which an alternative account can be built is the consideration of Thomas Heywood's dramatic career, which spanned the period from his work for Henslowe in the 1590s to work for Queen Anna's Men at the Red Bull and Cockpit in the early seventeenth century, and finally to his connection to Queen Henrietta's Men in the 1630s. The longevity of Heywood's career makes his work a crucial bridge between drama written over spatial and temporal divides and also the cultural gap that is assumed to hold between plays of amphitheatre and hall-playhouse provenance. The qualitative difference perceived between Red Bull and Cockpit plays is repeatedly appropriated in critical scholarship. R. A. McKee's unpublished MA thesis exemplifies some of the difficulties inherent in such an approach. McKee finds that "there [...] seem[s] to have been a more boisterous atmosphere on stage in the common theatre, matters being conducted more gracefully on the private stage" in accordance with the more sophisticated preferences of a higher-classed audience. Andrew Gurr's high-profile analysis corresponds to this perception, which suggests that the indoor playhouses "prefer witplay to swordplay", and recorders to trumpets. Some of these features are ascribed to the reduced performance spaces of the indoor playhouses, but in other cases they are repeatedly linked to discerning audience taste, in arguments that suggest that "the Cockpit provided for the gentry and their ladies, who wanted neither battles nor noise, let alone blood", or that: "the Cockpit stage had the poetry while the Red Bull had the fighting".[3] This rationale, which seeks to extrapolate knowledge of divergent audience preferences from the plays, commits to a variety of unverifiable assumptions: 1) that dramatists produced plays in accordance with recognisable tastes of a stable audience and in an identifiable demand-supply relationship; 2) that the raw thematic content and stage-directions of the play-texts suffice in themselves to offer knowledge of the play in performance; and, 3) that instances of spectacle and violence are indicative of preferences that are qualitatively opposed to moments of performance that deploy alternative

---

[3] Gurr, 'Singing Through the Chatter: Ford and Contemporary Theatrical Fashion', pp. 81-96.

methods of dramatic effect. The conclusions that these kinds of studies invite support the overbearing conviction that because audiences were socially bifurcated by economic distinctions, their tastes and preferences differed in direct proportion to their financial means: a difference that is expressed and ultimately encapsulated in the corpus of a company repertory. For Gurr, only plays of practical and aesthetic qualification are granted the privilege to transcend the social boundaries articulated by the amphitheatre/hall playhouse divide—a divide that he perceives as more pronounced than at any other time. In a discussion of plays that crossed from public to private playhouse, Gurr elucidates that not one contains any battle scenes, drum and trumpet calls, or duels.

In a paper given at the University of Birmingham's "Blurring the Boundaries" conference (September 2005), I have drawn attention to the extent to which this statement is a gross over-reduction—and dismissal—of the evidence. No less than five, full-scale battle scenes in *The Rape of Lucrece* were retained for performance at the Cockpit, and a third of amphitheatre plays that migrated to the Cockpit contain duels or fight scenes. Furthermore, swordplay was kept current on the Cockpit stage by its regular inclusion in new plays. Not only were Cockpit dramatists free enough from architectural determinism to revive Red Bull plays with their visual and physical interest intact, but they were prepared to do so in light of taste and fashion, as far as these came to bear upon dramatic production. The same can be said of visual effects such as gore, ghosts, godly descents, and the socialised spectacle of the rumbustious clowns.[4]

In practice, then, the Cockpit was regularly deploying old revivals and dramatic traditions, but cultural discourses that appear to have preoccupied playwrights at this time cast shadows over this repertory strategy, the outlines of which are dimly visible in the prefatory material and paratexts of the plays themselves. Ben Jonson's central position in the cultural debate over the value of theatrical and visual effects is well documented. In the prologue to *The Staple of News*, Jonson muses: "Would you were come to heare, not see a Play". He then expresses the author's wish to "have you wise,/Much rather by your eares, then by your eyes".[5] These statements invoke persistent oppositions between modes of theatrical engagement that privilege the auditory as it is filtered through "learned

---

[4] See Chettle's *Hoffman*, Ford's *Tis Pity She's a Whore*, and Kirke's *The Seven Champions of Christendom* for examples beyond the Heywood plays discussed here.

[5] Ben Jonson, lines 2, 5-6 of "The Prologue for the Stage" to *The Staple of News*, printed by I. B. for Robert Allot in 1631 with *Bartholomew Fair* and *The Devil is an Ass* (*EEBO*, accessed on 8th July 2007).

eares", over spectacle and its immediate appeal to the (implicitly unrefined) senses.[6] What is compelling about this debate is that it reveals the extent to which our modern constructions of dramatic types and corresponding audience types, are rooted in anxieties that began to dominate definitions of types of drama in the period and that stem from the suppliers of that drama itself.

In relation to this, I wish to draw attention to the issue of publication in this period and the impact that Benedict Scott Robinson has called "The cultural politics of play collections" might have had upon the content of prefatory material. Heywood's ambivalence towards the publication of plays is frequently cited.[7] He conspicuously draws attention to his uncertainty over the implications of printing. Eventually, he seems to change his mind and express an interest in publishing a "works", comprised of *The Ages* plays - but, conspicuously, this never materialises. Heywood's attitudes towards publication are now inextricably bound up in critical treatment of him as a dramatist, as a consequence of his particular sensitivity to publication. This suggests that he considered his work to be conspicuously implicated by the discourses governing the sale and artistic legitimisation of plays in book form—which included reference to their theatrical potential. Although this is beyond the scope of my argument, it is important to raise this methodological issue concerning constructions of readerships in the prefatory material, as opposed to theatrical audiences. Despite Heywood's professed quandary concerning whether to print his plays or not, he did, and it is important to recognise the extent to which the interpretation of the prologues must be managed through methodologies that remain alert to specific and cultural agendas according to the particular moment of publication, as well as performance.

Having said this, prologues nevertheless engage in constructions of dramatic traditions that correspond to particular imaginings of audience types. Moreover, the cultural work that they participate in is not diminished by the possibility that these prologues may never have been spoken on-stage—if anything, it makes them even more loaded. Heywood's continual engagement with shaping the reception of his drama

---

[6] Ben Jonson professes his hope that his play of *Cynthia's Revels* (first acted, as its title-page claims, in 1600, and published in 1601) will reach "learned ears", rather than a "vulgar and adul'trate Brain": this distinction is picked up on and satirised by Thomas Dekker in *Satiromastix* (published on the heels of *Cynthia's Revels*, in 1602). John Webster also begs a "full and understanding Auditory" in the note "To the Reader" of *The White Devil* (1612).

[7] See Brooks, *From Playhouse to Printing House: Drama and Authorship in Early Modern England* and Johnson, *The Actor as Playwright in Early Modern Drama*.

through constructing and privileging particular traditions and aspects of theatricality is connected, I would suggest, to his awareness within his long career of the social and cultural distinctions attached to writing for different audiences.

Crucially, the expectations that are attached to these distinctions are *never realised* or embodied by the drama that he actually produces. In the prologue to *The Royal King and Loyal Subject* (1637), Heywood associates theatrically fantastic representations with the past and its dramatic traditions, which, although aged, are figured as valuable and enriching tropes. Detailing his search for "invention" with which to furnish Chronicles that are otherwise "barren growne", Heywood writes that "no History/We have left unrifled, our Pens have, beene dipt/As well in opening each hid Manuscript".[8] Furthermore, Heywood invokes the discursive resonances of "high" and "low" culture in his imaginative sweep of the earth and heavens, in which he has "Div'd low as to the Center, and then reacht/Unto the Primum mobile above".[9] Significantly, he ascribes equal priority to both the elevated and subterranean reaches of invention. The extent to which Heywood is engaged with legitimising the familiar theatrical past and its possibilities for onstage representation in performance is reflected in the prologue's simultaneous invocation of a metaphor for creative writing, the recognition of rich dramatic traditions upon which playwrights could draw, and the connection of these with the physical representation of mythological characters such as the "Faiery Elves, Nymphs of the Sea and Land".[10] Heywood's threefold gathering of a classical past, theatrical history and the real-time experience of contemporary audiences is foregrounded most vividly in the opening of the prologue, which states that "The gods themselves we have brought downe to the Stage,/And figur'd them in Planets, made even Hell/ Deliver up the Furies".[11] This kind of address serves to connect past and present in the invocation of its physical embodiment in actual performance. The context of this prologue, presented before a play that is, within the context of Heywood's career, conspicuously lacking in theatrical representations of gods, furies, elves and nymphs, renders this conflation highly provocative.

Heywood's recognition of the need for "theatrical pleasure", as Nora

---

[8] Thomas Heywood, "The Prologue to the Stage" of *The Royal King and Loyal Subject*, in *The Dramatic Works of Thomas Heywood,* VI, pp. 3-83; lines 6-8; 14-15.

[9] Heywood, "Prologue": *Royal King and Loyal Subject*, lines 16-17.

[10] Heywood, "Prologue": *Royal King and Loyal Subject*, line 11.

[11] Heywood, "Prologue": *Royal King and Loyal Subject*, lines 2-4.

Johnson terms it, is evident once more in the prefatory matter to *The English Traveller* (1633). It is likewise a play that refrains to exploit the "Combate, Marriage, [...] Song, Dance, Masque, to bumbaste out a Play" that the prologue summons to the imagination.[12] Significantly, Heywood's prologue does not reject these performance spectacles on Jonson's grounds that such elements of spectacle fail to engage the "learned ear". Rather, Heywood qualifies his omissions with the acknowledgement that "Yet these [are] all good, and still in frequent use/With our best Poets", whilst gesturing towards the imagined reception of the anomalous: the "Strange Play you are like to have, for know,/We use no Drum, nor Trumpet, nor Dumbe show".[13] Instead, Heywood attributes this "defect" to "his selfe will" in response to his perception of the market's over-saturation of "so many" plays "in that kind".[14] The uncertainty that Heywood expresses in this prologue is manifest as he continues by stating that "He onely tries if once bare Lines will beare it", thus belying his anxiety over the theatrical potential of words alone.[15] Only one year later, his appropriation of the masque form, *Love's Mistress*, was in performance at court and on the Cockpit stage, the narrative framework of which is committed to working through these theatrical tensions.

The framing narrative of *Love's Mistress* functions as a para-text to the play as a whole, half-immersed in the world of the play, whilst maintaining a self-conscious distance from the fiction through its active engagement with qualifying and passing judgement on the drama itself. In this respect, I suggest that the framing narrative or chorus behaves as something like an extended prologue. It consists of an supplementary dialogue between Apuleius and Midas, interspersed between the main action of the play, in which they debate the artistic merit of particular dramatic types and the intellectual status of audiences. Here, Apuleius "seeks to advance / his Art" and is presented as a discerning marker of taste, whereas Midas is the "Mis-understanding" (1.1.466), "dull" and "covetous fool" (1.1.60), a clown figure, and vehicle for the debate between "Poetry" (1.1.409) and the kind of entertainment that Midas, the "King of beasts" (1.1.64), seeks.[16] Apuleius takes it upon himself to enlighten Midas and the audience of the play, and expresses his educative

---

[12] Thomas Heywood, "The Prologue" to *The English Traveller,* in *The Dramatic Works of Thomas Heywood*, IV, pp. 1-95; lines 3-4.
[13] Heywood, "Prologue: *The English Traveller*, lines 1-2; 5-6.
[14] Heywood, "Prologue: *The English Traveller*, lines 8-10.
[15] Heywood, "Prologue: *The English Traveller*, line 14.
[16] Thomas Heywood, *Love's Mistress*, in *The Dramatic Works of Thomas Heywood*, V, pp. 80-160.

programme in the introduction to the main body of the play, saying "Be you the Judges, we invite you all/Unto this banquet Accademicall" (1.1.85-6). Apuleius' artistic tastes are consistently contrasted with Midas'. During a dance featuring an "ignorant Asse" (*s.d.*1.1.446), Midas enquires: "What Reverend person's that of all the other? I like him best" (1.1.447). Apuleius answers dryly: "That Midas, is thy brother,/A piece of moving earth, illiterate, dull" (1.1.48-9). Both Apuleius and Midas ventriloquise the familiar narrative that "The vulgar are best pleas'd with noyse and showes" (3.1.381), a cultural delineation that implicates theatrical tradition and taste.

Constructions of desirable taste, then, are actively opposed to the on-stage presence of Midas as a clown-figure. At the same time, however, the obvious theatricality of Midas and his central role in the provision of real-time pleasure and the evocation of a popular dramatic tradition is exploited. The play's theatricality and narrative project depends, to an extent, upon the continued presence of the clown-figure on-stage, even while his theatrical legitimacy and tastes are ridiculed. The continued currency of the clown on-stage as a consequence of the working-through of debates over taste places him in a unique position within *Love's Mistress*—as an indispensable narrative and dramatic device through which theatrical traditions and artistic preferences are negotiated but which, at the same time, constitutes and embodies one of the traditions, as an implicit reflection of audience taste, that is itself being contested.

This tension between the narrative construction of Midas' artistic preferences and their real-time theatrical potential is revealed again when Midas begs Apuleius to "let me shew thee some of our fine sport" (i.e., the dance [2.1.370]). Apuleius reluctantly acquiesces, condescending that "Art some-times must give way to ignorance" (2.1.375), even though he himself exploits this contrived dance as part of his cultural programme. The blurring of the boundaries between "ignorant" entertainment, and educative art destabilises any sharp distinction between the traditions at stake in this debate. Therefore, the value of the entertainment provided by Midas' dance is recognised by the theatrical pleasure it provides to an audience, peripheral to the narrative of the play proper. Later, the contest between Pan and Apollo is staged, in which a clown figure sings on behalf of Pan. Here, Midas is brought out of the liminal space of the Chorus frame and into the main action, as an arbiter of taste. The Clown's performance of the song is ridiculed by Apollo, who draws attention to its rusticity in the scorn that "Henceforth be all your rurall musicke such,/Made out of Tinkers, Pans, and Kettle-drums" (3.1.202-3). In a familiar construction of responsibility over the audience's reception of the contest, he asserts that "what's amisse/Is not in us, but in their ignorance" (3.1.215-6). Yet through the staging of the contest – a specific inflection of the cultural debate over the legitimacy of theatrical traditions and their reception by a vulgar audiences – there consists a recognition of the pleasure that the Clown's song is able to provide, which in part depends upon the construction of its rusticity. This corresponds to the dependence that Heywood confers upon the theatrical past and its dramatic devices in the prologue to *The Royal King and Loyal Subject*.

In this essay, I've explored the gap between what Heywood's prologues and paratexts claim the plays are doing and what the plays actually are doing. In *Love's Mistress,* tastes and traditions are negotiated, but with little impact upon what audiences were seeing performed. Similarly, the prologues work to construct and reconcile the cultural and aesthetic boundaries of "high" and "low" artistic taste, based upon the identification of "spectacle" and the use of "out-dated" dramatic traditions. The implied continuity in taste across Heywood's plays goes some way towards providing a model to account for the means by which repertories could be managed. It thereby reveals the potential cohesion that amalgamated repertories—such as that of Queen Henrietta's Men—could command within a competitive and commercial theatrical environment. But to demand this kind of cohesion from a corpus of plays is to force the repertory study to perform links and account for consistencies within a corpus of plays through the invocation of "intention" on the part of dramatists and company managers. A study of Heywood's career, which includes work for both theatre "types" and audiences, provides the starting point for a methodology that seeks to examine the relationship of the dramatist to the construction of commercial repertories. This is a process which, as the prefatory matter and prologues to the plays suggest, is inextricably bound to discourses of taste; the audience projection and the creation of divisions between repertories; the theatres and corresponding notions of the worth of art in this period; and the perception that the location of a theatre governed the content of its plays. These distinctions have traditionally governed the shape of current theatre history narratives and shaped the reception and interpretation of the plays. Heywood's professional interest in reconciling the discourses of high and low artistic traditions across audiences and repertories as well as controlling the reception of his plays is indicative of a dramatists' negotiation and legitimisation of not only the aesthetic framework in which his work was - and is - to be located, but the works' implications for the commercial operation of the repertory of Queen Henrietta's Men.

Works Cited

The Dramatic Works of Thomas Heywood. 6 vols. London: John Pearson, 1874.

All other early-modern texts referenced have been accessed on "Early English Books Online", at http://eebo.chadwyck.com/home.

Bentley, G. E. *The Jacobean and Caroline Stage.* 7 vols. London: Oxford University Press, 1941-1968.

Bergeron, David. *Textual Patronage in English Drama, 1570-1640.* Aldershot: Ashgate, 2006.

Brooks, Douglas. *From Playhouse to Printing House: Drama and Authorship in Early Modern Culture.* Cambridge: Cambridge University Press, 2000.

Bruster, Douglas and Robert Weimann. *Prologues to Shakespeare's Theatre: Performance and Liminality in Early Modern Drama.* London: Routledge, 2004.

Gurr, Andrew. *Playgoing in Shakespeare's London.* Cambridge: Cambridge University Press, 1987.

—. *The Shakespearian Playing Companies.* Oxford: Clarendon Press, 1996.

—. "Singing Through the Chatter: Ford and Contemporary Theatrical Fashion." In *John Ford: Critical Revisions* ed. by Michael Neill. Cambridge: Cambridge University Press, 1988.

Johnson, Nora. *The Actor as Playwright in Early Modern Drama.* Cambridge: Cambridge University Press, 2003.

Knutson, Roslyn. *The Repertory of Shakespeare's Company 1594-1613.* Fayetteville: University of Arkansas Press, 1991.

Lesser, Zachary and Alan B. Farmer. "Vile Arts: The Marketing of English Printed Drama, 1512-1660". In *Research Opportunities for Renaissance Drama* 39 (2000) 77-165.

McKee, R. A. "Thomas Heywood's Plays and the Tastes of his Audiences", unpublished MA Thesis, The Shakespeare Institute, 1972.

Orgel, Stephen. "The Poetics of Spectacle." In *New Literary History: A Journal of Theory and Interpretation*, 2:3 (1971), 367-389.

Reynolds, George F. *The Staging of Elizabethan Plays at The Red Bull Theatre, 1605-1625.* London and New York: Oxford University Press and the Modern Language Association of America, 1940.

Stern, Tiffany. *Making Shakespeare: From Stage to Page.* Routledge: London, 2004.

Weimann, Robert. "Performance-Game and Representation in *Richard III.*" In *Textual and Theatrical Shakespeare: Questions of Evidence,* ed. by Edward Pechter. Iowa City: University of Iowa Press, 1996.

Wiles, David. *Shakespeare's Clown: Actor and Text in the Elizabethan Playhouse.* Cambridge: Cambridge University Press, 1987.

Worthen, W. B. *Shakespeare and the Authority of Performance.* Cambridge: Cambridge University Press, 1997.

CHAPTER THREE

BAWDINESS, CRIME AND LOW CHARACTERS IN LATE ELIZABETHAN COMEDY

SHELLY HSIN-YI HSIEH

This paper focuses on characters of low birth in late Elizabethan comedy who are caricatured as moral transgressors or victims of sexual offences committed by the upper class.[1] The historical and literary contexts of the Elizabethan period provide information on immoral acts committed by people from all social stratums who had failed to bridle their passion, of which two specific corpuses of materials will be investigated in this article. Presentments in relation to "sexual aberration" are the main category of Essex Archidiaconal records, and the delineation of sexual offences also prevails in late Elizabethan comedy.[2] Such a correspondence between common transgressions presented before church courts and popular episodes enacted on the Elizabethan stage might reveal a significant influence of social "anxiety" on the development of humorous and theatrical subjects. However, rather than investigating specific cases of sexual offences to which the playwrights of late Elizabethan comedy were keen to respond precisely, this paper shall instead, by juxtaposing literary instances with the immorality cases of Essex County Records, attempt to pinpoint what kind of social phenomena, as a whole, had underpinned most playwrights' thought of achieving a connection between bawdy

---

[1] The composed or performed years of the plays discussed in this paper are based on the assumptions in Harbage's *Annuals of English Drama: 975-1700*.
[2] Emmison, *Elizabethan Life: Morals & The Church Courts*, p. 1; among the modern collections of the historical facts with regard to sexual offences committed by the commoners, Emmison's research on Essex Archidiaconal Records serves as a more unified body of extant records.

characters and lowly life. Yet in making a comparison among the supposed immoral characters presented by John Lyly, William Shakespeare, Thomas Dekker and Ben Jonson, it is interesting to note that while these playwrights were presented with a shared contemporary impression of "popular" sexual offences, such as premarital sex and pregnancy, adultery, and prostitution, a distinction can nonetheless be found in their work between the attitudes of boys and adults, females and males, servile workers and gentlemen, and the punishment they face for their misdemeanours.

The Elizabethan community placed great emphasis on moral reformation. Only marriage could justify sex. Thus, unlike an accusation of adultery in a modern sense, there was little difference between premarital sex and an affair after marriage. Despite a betrothal, engaged couples who had consummated their passion before a nuptial ritual were likely to be accused of sexual offences and also sent to church courts. The church courts did deal with cases besides sexual offences, for example, drunkenness, swearing and defamation, nonetheless, as F. G. Emmison notes, "[b]ecause the various sex charges were so commonplace in the archidiaconal courts, they were by a natural corollary, known in vulgar parlance throughout England as the Bawdy courts".[3]

Modern scholarship suspects that low and poor people might have suffered more from the social standard for morality. According to J. A. Sharp, "[i]t remains problematic whether these collective notions [of proper behaviour] were those of the 'community' or of its ruling stratum of relatively rich and perhaps relatively respectable yeomen and artisans".[4] Consequently, a poor offender who was neither literate, nor had money to afford redemption or bribe an officer, might face the danger of being wrongfully accused of offences.[5] This hierarchal order is hinted at in *The Merry Wives of Windsor* (1597), where the commoners', as well as the women's, revenge on an upper-class sexual offender is presented alongside a juxtaposition of the influential middle class and a lustful knight with

---

[3] Emmison, *Morals*, p. 2.
[4] Sharp, *Crimes in Early Modern England 1550-1750*, p. 119.
[5] As "formalised in the reign of Henry VII", the so-called "benefit of clergy" was applicable to "those convicted of felony, notably theft and manslaughter" who "might escape hanging on a first conviction if they could read"; in order to prevent some offenders from abusing this benefit, "[c]ertain offences, notably murder with malice aforethought and rape, never lay within the scope of clergy, while later legislation rendered a number of crimes, among them burglary, sodomy, bestiality, witchcraft and horse-theft, non-clergyable" (Sharp 95).

moribund authority. Before playwrights of city comedy took such a reversed power structure as a humorous and dramatic subject, a double attitude towards the poor or powerless sexual offenders had already become commonplace in Elizabethan society.

A double attitude also existed in the expected age of newly-weds. Although The Statute of Artificers of 1563, urged people who were "under the age of thirty years" to get married, those who were still bound as apprentices or servile men, alongside those who were under twenty-four years old, were not eligible to commence marital life.[6] In this view, marriage became not only a ticket but also a barrier to sex. While men and women's curiosity about carnal knowledge would have developed since the age of puberty, officially many of them from the lower stratum of society had to remain abstinent until they completed apprenticeships and became mature enough or had adequate wealth to be freed from service. Even so, servant-maid intercourse, resulting from growing curiosity and physical need, was not unusual in an Elizabethan household. Furthermore, as they were living under the same roof and even sleeping in the same bedroom, some of the supposed household governors were also inclined to have affairs with their dependents. Although masters and mistresses might also fail to keep their sexual desire in control, they had been authorised to discipline their employees and were responsible for any transgression committed by their subordinates. When servants, whether male or female, were eventually accused of immorality and waited to be whipped or enjoined to perform penance, church courts usually assigned their employers to carefully guard the offenders at home in case they might run away before punishment was administered. Nevertheless, the employers, afraid of being incriminated or bringing public reproach upon themselves, preferred to remove this household disgrace as soon as possible.

If we compare this with the literary world, boy and young male servants who temporarily quit their service or worry about being discharged are commonly found in Lyly's plays, which were written for court entertainment and performed by boy actors. Consequently, rather than a desire for sex, it is victuals as necessities of life, together with gold as a means to pursue a better life, which are of more concern to Lylian servants; hunger is hence pinpointed as the main cause of boys' dissatisfaction with their servile condition. That these fictional boys are insensitive to sex might be either a conscious decision to depict them as

---

[6] "Statute of Artificers of 1563 or An Act touching divers orders for artificers, labourers, servants of husbandry and apprentices", (Prothero, 4), 45-54 (46).

too young to realise their sexual need or because Lyly was so afraid of incurring Queen Elizabeth's disfavour that he preferred not to make his boys perform bawdily before the authority. In Lyly's last play, *The Woman in the Moon* (1590), Gunophilus is punished because he has tried to abscond with household jewels and elope with his mistress, Pandora. But Gunophilus divulges that his transgression is not done because of love but a servant's obedience as he "was ne'er in love with her" until she becomes deranged in Act V.[7] In other words, he is commanded by Pandora to cuckold his master rather than be motivated by his own desire to commit adultery.

By comparison with boy characters, Lylian maidservants are imbued with more sexual knowledge. Bawdy jokes and servant-maid intercourse are touched on in *Mother Bombie* (1590), wherein Rixula's identity as an "experienced" maidservant is hinted at in Mother Bombie's soothsaying when Rixula is looking for her "spoon": "Thy spoon is not stolen but mislaid./Thou art an ill housewife although a good maid./Look for thy spoon where thou hadst like to be no maid".[8] Mother Bombie's pun on "maid" and "spoon" reminds Rixula of her sexual life, but Halfpenny, as a boy servant, seems too innocent to solve this riddle:

Halfpenny. Wert thou once put to it?
Rixula. No, sir boy, it was put to me.

Paying much attention to the lexical denotation of "put to", "Halfpenny asks if somebody put her up to stealing the spoon" for in Halfpenny's respect it is simply a kitchen utensil. Due to such mutual misapprehension, Rixula "replies with the still-current slang phrase 'put to', as 'put it to her,' for sexual intercourse".[9] Maidservants' pre-nuptial sex entailed a social contempt, but Rixula seems too young to take it seriously. G. K. Hunter presumes that "*Mother Bombie* would seem to be for boys not for court, *The Woman in the Moon* for court but not for boys".[10] The former lacks a

---

[7] Lyly, *The Woman in the Moon* in *The Plays of John Lyly*, ed. by Daniel, p. 353; According to Harbage and relevant modern scholarship, Lyly's *The Woman in the Moon* was written around 1593, but Leah Scragg deconstructs this long-time presumption and argues that "*The Woman in the Moon* was written prior to the closure of Paul's Boys", namely circa 1590, in *Lyly: The Woman in the Moon*, ed. by Scragg, pp. 8-9.

[8] Lyly, *Mother Bombie*, 3.4, Daniel, 266.

[9] *Ibid.*, note 124, Daniel, 379.

[10] Hunter, *John Lyly: the Humanist as Courtier*, p. 83.

record of its performance at court while the latter has unknown auspices and is thus suspected as a play performed by adults. If Hunter's supposition is reliable, it seems that Lyly's court career had been moribund before boy performances were completely stopped approximately in the year 1590. Thus, the description of Rixula's sexual experience and Gunophilus's interaction with his mistress might suggest that Lyly, although keeping his low characters childish, had gradually joined his late plays to a commercial repertoire of an adult company.

In contrast to the fictional Rixula, who is ignorant of any punishment of her sexual offences, in actuality a hired maid who was unmarried and pregnant, or merely suspected of having an illicit relationship, invariably had to face more danger than her male counterpart. Contemporary church-court accusations and public disapproval of pre-nuptial sex and pregnancy might cause the female offenders to be discharged from household service. In acknowledgment of this social warning, Shakespearean low-ranking male characters, in contrast to Lylian boys, are adults more aware of the danger of committing sexual offences, yet Shakespearean low female characters, though sexually active, remain silent when the truth is out.

In *Love's Labour's Lost* (1595), Costard, who serves as an example of being "taken/with a wench", fails to defend his innocence, yet is only sentenced to "fast/a week with bran and water" although the proclaimed penalty is "a year's imprisonment" (1.1.276-289). Though unable even to fend for himself, Costard worries about Jaquenetta, the country wench who he is accused of staying with, but who we later learn is actually involved with Don Adriano De Armado; in Act 5 Scene 2, either divulging a truth, or for the purpose of poking fun at his rival, Costard denounces Armado's dishonour and angrily states that the "poor wench is cast away. She's quick. The child brags/in her belly already. 'Tis yours" (5.2.669-70). With love and pity for Jaquenetta, Costard later comically devotes himself to waging a life-and-death battle with Armado, who is eager to accuse Costard of defamation so as to protect his honour. Throughout this heated debate, as well as Costard's witty defence against the accusation in Act 1 Scene 1, Shakespeare does not provide Jaquenetta an opportunity to explain whether she has committed sexual offences and who with.

The contrasting silence of Jaquenetta is echoed throughout Shakespeare's early comedies; and, when it came to the second half of the 1590s, the silence or absence of a female character was especially emphasised at the last moment of a play. In *Much Ado About Nothing* (1598), although Leonato commands the watch to arrange a courtroom confrontation between Margaret and her paramour, such a scene does not take place. Margaret is accused when she is absent in Act 5 Scene 1, and then her offence is simply pardoned in Leonato's few-line narration in Act 5 Scene 4 when she, albeit on stage, remains silent. Correspondingly, in *Twelfth Night* (1601), although witty, Maria disappears after Act 4; her trick played on Malvolio, together with her affair with Sir Toby Belch, is only remarked by Fabian in Act 5.

In addition to their subsequent silence, the offences of Jaquenetta, Margaret, and Maria are also connected in their shared desire to change their low condition by being wooed by a gentleman. Yet while the offences committed by these three maids are similar, the consequences of their moral transgressions distinguish them from each other. Jaquenetta, who is the only one living beyond court, the most innocent, and least witty of the three, is cast away by her employer, which reflects a common case in Elizabethan circumstances. Margaret is accused but pardoned in the end, which pinpoints the possibility that the lawsuit can be withdrawn, while Maria is supposed to marry into the upper class without any accusation of her earlier offences.

While the female characters are tried for sexual offences, the low male characters in Shakespeare's early comedies, like Costard, merely touch on a sexual issue, for example, the two Dromio(s) in *The Comedy of Errors* (1592), Launce in *The Two Gentlemen of Verona* (1593), and artisans in *A Midsummer Night's Dream* (1595), but these adult parts, albeit bawdy, pay little attention to their sexual lust. In *The Comedy of Errors*, Dromio of Syracuse enters Act 3 Scene 2 running hastily. He has mistakenly been chased by Luce, Adriana's kitchen maid, because of the confusion resulting from the twin servants. After Dromio avoids this sexual seduction, Luce is bawdily described in his conversation with Antipholus of Syracuse. Nevertheless, there is no physical interaction between either of the twin Dromios and the supposed lustful maid in the play. Similarly, in *Two Gentlemen of Verona*, a bride's dowry rather than her virginal charm is of more interest to Launce. The strength and weakness of this would-be wife is well discussed by Launce and Speed, but she never physically appears on stage.

Conversely, gossip about a man's indulgence in carnal pleasure is hinted at in *A Midsummer Night's Dream*. In Act 1 Scene 2, Peter Quince pinpoints Bottom's sexual lust by referring to Bottom's suggestion of wearing a "French-crown-coloured-beard" to its connotation of contracting venereal diseases, which is also taken as a sexual offence of the period (1.2.88-91). However, by comparison with Bottom's little attention to Quince's jesting about his sexuality, Bottom becomes more serious about his forest confrontation with Titania. In Act 4 Scene 1, Bottom therefore concludes that his moral transgression, as well as seduction by a fairy queen, is merely a dream.

It is difficult to assume how far there could be a connection between the law of the period and Bottom's hesitation in revealing his bizarre affair to his comrades, yet other characters of the period do recognise the law. A male character from the lower stratum of society who worries about being accused of such an offence is more directly presented in *As You Like It* (1599), when Touchstone realises the importance of marriage; if Audrey and he are not lawfully married, they "must live in bawdry".[11] Preceding Touchstone's warning to Audrey, the danger of being involved in an illicit relationship has been illustrated in George Chapman's *The Comedy of Humours* (1597), in which Verone, the host of an alehouse, attempts to seduce his maid. At the end of the play, he is presented before the king and jestingly accused of causing his maid to be "great with child". Verone endevours to deny the suspected liaison and concludes that he has been abused for the purpose of pleasing the king.[12] Whether Verone has committed an illegal sex act or not, the above accusation adumbrates another two sexual offences: harbouring an unmarried mother and bastardy. The former is with regard to "those who ... gave accommodation, temporarily or otherwise, to harlots, vagrants or other women".[13] The latter is undeniable evidence to prosecute someone for premarital sex. "[M]any more alehouse-keepers were in trouble than their customers, unless they were vagrants"; besides encouraging people to indulge in drinking, alehouse-keepers who were "lodging women about to give birth to bastards" were also against the law.[14]

Another large category of sexual offences in Essex Archidiaconal records is prostitution. Similar to the predicament of the alehouse-keepers, "the brothel-keepers rather than the strumpets and their customers" were of more concern to church courts.[15] A prostitute was also called a brothel until the term "brothel-house" which had never been used in court records became known to Elizabethans on other occasions nearer the turn of the

---

[11] Shakespeare, *As You Like It*, 3.3.79-80, Greenblatt 1634.
[12] Chapman, *An Humorous Day's Mirth or The Comedy of Humour*, D4^v, H1^r.
[13] Emmison, *Moral*, p. 25.
[14] Emmison, *Elizabethan Life: Disorder*, pp. 212, 203.
[15] Emmison, *Morals*, p. 24.

seventeenth century.[16] In Elizabethan comedy, it is more common to present a courtesan or prostitute as a synthesis of a bawd and brothel, and her lodging is certainly taken as a bawdy house. Besides Lamia in George Whetstone's *Promos and Cassandra* (1578) and Lais in Lyly's *Campaspe* (1583), the nameless courtesan in *The Comedy of Errors* is another pertinent example, where a prostitute of this sort is described as the source of spiritual vice and venereal diseases. As soon as the courtesan approaches Antipholus and Dromio of Syracuse, these two men attempt to distance themselves from her so as to avoid being exposed to infection which might not only corrupt a man's morality but also deprive him of physical health:

> **Antipholus of Syracuse.** Satan, avoid! I charge thee, tempt me not!
> **Dromio of Syracuse.** Master, is this Mistress Satan?
> **Antipholus of Syracuse.** It is the devil.
> **Dromio of Syracuse.** Nay, she is worse, she is the devil's dam, and here she comes in the habit of a light wench. And thereof comes that the wenches say, "God damn me;" that's as much as to say, "God make me a light wench." It is written, they appear to men like angels of light. Light is an effect of fire, and fire will *burn*. Ergo, light wenches will *burn*. Come not near her (4.3.49-57).

Whereas the courtesan's immorality piques Antipholus of Syracuse's attention, the word "burn" is of great concern to his Dromio, who seems more familiar with such a medical and also courtroom term with regard to "venereal diseases", which indeed bear a relation to prostitution. According to the earliest mention of "burning", "'heating and filthiness' of the penis" could occur because of "lying with a[n] unclean woman".[17] Sexual offences of this type, whether to be burnt by someone or to cause someone to burn, were common cases presented before church courts; consequently, "apart from the single case referring to the 'pocks' and a woman 'greatly diseased', all the entries use the term 'burned'".[18] Once such offences were confirmed, the offenders had to be purified in a medical as well as religious way. "The record book of a St. Botolph-without-Aldgate, London, parish clerk gives syphilis as the probable cause of twelve deaths in 1585-99"; thus venereal diseases, although not resulting in as many deaths as the plague, were undoubtedly

---

[16] *Ibid.*, 20.
[17] "The earliest mention of burning apparently occurs in Guy de Chauliac's *Chirurgia magna* (1363)", Emmison, *Morals*, p. 32.
[18] Emmison, *Morals*, p. 32.

dangerous for an individual and society.[19] Other terms in relation to infamous contagions, such as "Pox" and "French crown", are frequently adopted by less civil characters in late Elizabethan comedy to curse or poke fun at their comrades and enemies. The playwrights of the period hardly touched on the actual issue of venereal diseases. "Shakespeare was one of the very few literary writers who adopted the verb: [burn]"; he also presented an occasion to illustrate a symptom of syphilis in *A Midsummer Night's Dream*.[20] From Dromio's fear of being burnt and Quince's suggestion that Bottom has been already burnt to a mere language for mocking or cursing each other, these instances highlight not only social disapproval but also a stereotyped impression of lowly life in which the fashion of prostituting oneself, acting as a whoremaster and delivering ill terms prevail any moral concern. The above instances, however, understate the seriousness of this offence and imply that it might occur as commonly as a trivial mistake.

Calling people adulterers, cuckolds or other implicit images of bawdy terms might also incur an accusation of slander which overlapped defamation. It was not unusual that an employee slandered his or her employer, but whether he or she would be sent to church courts depended on their daily relationships. In a comedy, a servant's slanderous languages are hardly taken as serious offences against his master. For example, in Dekker's *The Shoemaker's Holiday* (1599), Simon Eyre's journeyman, Firk, repeatedly plays a pun on "horns" and "cuckoldry", but Eyre as the supposed target of slander is not irritated because "the jest was so conventional that even from a man to his master it probably did not seem offensive".[21]

Conversely, a husband in a city comedy who suspects that he has been shamed by prostitution is usually determined to revenge himself on the supposed adulterers, despite the seducer's social degree. In Jonson's *Every Man in His Humour* (1598), Cob, a water-bearer, accuses his wife, Tib, of adultery and beats her without any hesitation.[22] Shifting from the Italian

---

[19] T. R. Forbes, *Chronicle from Aldgate* (Yale Univ., 1971), 101-106, quoted by Emmison, in *Morals*, p. 36.

[20] See note 24.

[21] Thomas Dekker, *The Shoemaker's Holiday*, ed. by R. L. Smallwood and Stanley Wells, sc. 1.166; note 166, p. 92.

[22] Ben Jonson, *Every Man in his Humour*, ed. by Robert S. Miola, 5.2.83-96; *Everyman in His Humour* was first produced in 1598, published in 1601; it was revised sometime afterwards and published in the folio of 1616; the edition of The Revels Plays is based on the quarto version of 1601.

settings to the London surroundings, Cob in the revised edition (1601-1616) further pinpoints Kitely, a merchant, as Tib's paramour and is eager to present them before the judge.[23] Although the accusation proves a mistake, it seems that the suspect's financial condition could not alter an angry husband's determination. However, given the fact that "the gentry usually had the privilege of not being sued in the local courts", a husband who is of common birth and supposed to be cuckolded in a comedy seldom resorts to the law if his rival in love belongs to the gentry.[24] On the contrary, he prefers to chastise such a transgressor in private. In addition to *The Merry Wives of Windsor*, another instance is shown in *The Shoemaker's Holiday* in which Ralph Damport, together with his shoemaker comrades, claims his wife back by threatening Master Hammon, a city gentleman, who has almost deceived her into remarrying him.

Apart from the common types of sexual offences, it is interesting to note that "the wearing of men's clothes by females of a lewd or lively disposition" was recorded in many cases of incontinence.[25] In 1585, a "Littlebury woman 'did wear man's apparel disorderly in her master's house'".[26] It is unclear whether a female transvestite was accused because of her cross-dressing or because of implications of homosexuality, but the remaining cases in this category show an obvious relation to offences of adultery. It seems that disguise became means for a woman, whether married or unmarried, to procure secret intercourse with her paramour. The term "tomboy" and "coat" are comically connected in a conversation between page boys and a maidservant in Lyly's *Midas* (1589):

> **Licio.** … What news?
> **Pipenetta.** I would not be in your *coats* for anything.
> **Licio.** Indeed, if thou shouldst rig up and down in our *jackets*, thou wouldst be thought a very *tomboy*.
> **Pipenetta.** I mean I would not be in your *case*.[27]

In misunderstanding Pipenetta's connotation of "coat" which means "circumstance" on this occasion, Licio relates this word to its apparent

---

[23] *The Mermaid Series: Ben Jonson*, ed. by Brinsley Nicholson and C. H. Herford, vol. 1, pp. 95-6; the Mermaid edition is based on the revised version.
[24] Emisson, *Morals*, p. 6.
[25] Emmison, *Morals*, 18.
[26] *Ibid.*
[27] Lyly, *Midas*, 1.2, Daniel 206.

meaning, "jacket", and points out how dishonorable she will be thought if found putting on male clothes. A boy actor cast in a female part, whether in disguise or not, created a strong dramatic effect when juxtaposed with an adult actor, who was cast in a male part. By the 1590s, disguise of female characters had become a theatrical fashion. Many heroines in the comedies of the period are motivated by love or other grounds to disguise themselves as youths, but most of them feel shame at being ostensibly cross-gendered.

The evidence from court cases and the discussed plays demonstrate that while social degrees of sexual offenders could influence the consequence and process of trial, the traditional superiority of males to females did not influence whether an immorality case should be presented or withdrawn. However, wanton women were supposed to be less acceptable than incontinent men to patriarchal society; thus, some indictments on sexual offences only applied to female offenders, and the playwrights appear to emphasise the sexual acts of women above the bawdy inclinations of men. Those who engaged in a brothel business, cuckolded a husband, and delivered a bastard, whether married or unmarried, certainly suffered from much social disapproval, as reflected in the drama of the time. The consequences of these offences were feared as harmful not only to the order of the whole society but to the right of the individual as well.

Works Cited

Chapman, George. *An Humorous Day's Mirth* or *The Comedy of Humours*. 1597 *Early English Books Online*, 1475-1640. Microfilm STC1/ Reel 190:15.

Dekker, Thomas. *The Shoemaker's Holiday*. The Revels Plays. Eds. & Intro. R. L. Smallwood and Stanley Wells. Manchester and New York: Manchester UP, 1999.

Emisson, F. G. *Elizabethan Life: Disorder*. Chelmsford: Essex County Council, 1970.

—. *Elizabethan Life: Morals & The Church Courts*. Chelmsford: Essex County Council, 1973.

Harbage, Alfred. *Annals of English Drama: 975-1700*. Rev. S. Schoenbaum. 2nd ed. London: Methuen, 1964.

Hunter, G. K. *John Lyly: the Humanist as Courtier*. London: Routledge & Kegan Paul, 1962.

Jonson, Ben. *Every Man in his Humour. The Mermaid Series: Ben Jonson.* 3 vols. Vol. 1. Eds. & Intro. Brinsley Nicholson and C. H. Herford. London; New York: T. Fisher Unwin; Charles Scribner's Sons, 1908.

—. *Every Man in his Humour.* The Revels Plays. Ed. & intro. Robert S. Miola. Manchester: Manchester UP, 1988, 2000.

Lyly, John. *Midas. The Plays of John Lyly.* Ed. & Intro. Carter A. Daniel. Lewisburg; London and Toronto: Bucknell UP; Associated UP, 1988. 200-37

—. *Campaspe.* Daniel 30-64

—. *Mother Bombie.* Daniel 242-84

—. *The Woman in the Moon.* Daniel 318-60

—. *The Woman in the Moon.* The Revels Plays. Ed. & Intro. Leah Scragg. Manchester: Manchester UP, 2006.

Prothero, G. W., ed. 'Statute of Artificers of 1563 or An Act touching divers orders for artificers, labourers, servants of husbandry and apprentices'. *Select Statutes and Other Constitutional Documents Ilustrative of the Reigns of Elizabeth and James I.* 4th ed. Oxford: Clarendon 1913, 1924, 1934.

Shakespeare, William. *A Midsummer Night's Dream. The Norton Shakespeare.* Gen. Ed. & Intro. Stephen Greenblatt. New York: Norton, 1997. 814-61

—. *As You Like It.* Greenblatt 1600-56

—. *The Comedy of Errors.* Greenblatt 690-730

—. *The Love's Labour's Lost.* Greenblatt 741-800

—. *The Merry Wives of Windsor.* Greenblatt 1234-89

—. *Much Ado About Nothing.* Greenblatt 1389-443

—. *Twelfth Night.* Greenblatt 1768-821

—. *The Two Gentlemen of Verona.* 1593. Greenblatt 84-130

Sharp, J. A. *Crime in Early Modern England 1550-1750.* London and New York: Longman, 1984, 1999.

Whetstone, George. *Promos and Cassandra, Part 1 & 2. Old English Drama: Student's Facsimile Edition.* Reproduced in Facsimile, 1910.

Chapter Four

Print and Elizabethan Military Culture

Dong-Ha Seo

I

As early as the sixteenth century Western Europe faced a dramatic reformation of the ways in which the soldiers were raised and organised as well as the ways in which wars were fought. Military historians have considered changes in strategy, tactics and weapons technology during the sixteenth and seventeenth centuries to be revolutionary.[1] One of the most significant military developments was the use of firearms and artillery. Particularly gunpowder, as Francis Bacon perceived, revolutionarily contributed to the changes of conditions of war:

> [I]t is worth while to notice the force, virtue, and consequences of discoveries. And these appear more manifestly in none than in those three…Printing, Gunpowder, and the Needle. For these three have changed the face and state of things in all the world: the first in letters, the second, in war, the third, in navigation.[2]

Along with gunpowder, it was print, as Elizabeth Eisenstein puts it, "an agent of change", that had an enormous impact on every field of human experience since the Renaissance.[3] Both gunpowder and print were instrumental in the intellectual and military revolutions of the Renaissance.

Yet, whereas it was thought by the Elizabethans that printing brought about the most radical transformation in the conditions of intellectual life, gunpowder, having inhuman destructiveness, was accused of increasing

---

[1] Parker, *The Military Revolution: Military Innovation and the Rise of the West 1500-1800.*
[2] Bacon, *The Novum Organon or A True Guide to the Interpretation of Nature*, p. 110.
[3] Eisenstein, *The Printing Press an Agent of Change.*

the size of armies and the cost of war.[4] It was these destructive conditions of modern warfare which reduced soldiers to "food for powder" (*1H4* 4.2.65). But despite the contradictory characteristics, a close affiliation developed between gunpowder and printing during the Renaissance. For example, when William Camden recorded an account of the history of printing, he juxtaposed the impact of gunpowder with that of the printing press: "[as] gunnes were invented to destruction, so shortly after was the arte of printing found to the conservation and restoringe of learning".[5] Using the opposing natures between gunpowder and printing, both Bacon and Camden as men of letters emphasised the significance of printing which was taking part in construction of knowledge; their narratives, listing both printing and gunpowder together, provide a hint of a newly developed alliance between printing and military subjects during this period.

II

The transitional approach to the Elizabethan military world has witnessed the series of changes which took place in Continental warfare, while England remained a deeply insular country and was behind the Continent in military revolution.[6] Specifically, the Elizabethan army, long overlooked in favour of the more spectacular achievement of its navy, was consequently seen as a military backwater with much to improve from the great changes in modern warfare. Although Elizabethan England was comparatively unaffected by the Continental warfare, there was enough activity to produce numerous military subject books which became cultural phenomena. The relationship between printing and military penetrated the Elizabethans' imagination, and the proliferation of military subject books ensured that the subject was not limited to the persons or places in which war were actually being fought. Hence, in this paper, I will suggest that Elizabethan military books printed during the late sixteenth and early seventeenth centuries attracted Elizabethan readers not only because of the series of wars in which they were involved, but also because of the close association between printing and military culture.

During the last two decades of Queen Elizabeth's reign, England was involved in wars in Ireland, Spain and the Low Countries and large

---

[4] Eisenstein 107; Hale, *War and Society in Renaissance Europe*, pp. 46-7.
[5] Camden, *Remains Concerning Britain,* p. 147.
[6] As for the English military organisation and personnel, see both foundational studies such as Cruickshank, *Elizabeth's Army* and Boynton, *The Elizabethan Militia.*

numbers of men were recruited or impressed for military service. Unsurprisingly, Elizabethans were interested in the accounts of the various campaigns. In the absence of newspapers, it has previously been thought that the Elizabethans were at best satisfied with tales told by returned soldiers and sailors in taverns or inns. However, recent studies suggest that printed texts of first-hand military experience served not only to supply much needed information of war to the general public, but also to shape a militaristic-minded audience during the years of the Elizabethan wars.[7] Furthermore, tackling the issue beyond contemporary dramatic representation, Curtis C. Breight argues that along with dramatic fiction, Elizabethan military discourses were purposely shaped by and circulated through the government's policy, the theoretical conceptualisations of warfare in military treatises and propagandic sermons.[8] However, despite the preoccupation with military subjects in various genres, our understanding of the period, and the Elizabethan army as small and hardly significant, can mislead us to see even a "sudden deluge" of military book publication during this period as the writers' attempts either to seek protection amongst the chief nobles against threat from censorship, or merely to add lustre to their name by association with the men in power.[9] Naturally, it fails to explain how far Elizabethan audiences and readers experienced militarism in the context of military culture. However, when we examine book publications of the period, rather than a standard portrait of Elizabethan army's ineffectiveness, we clearly see how significantly Elizabethan military culture through the printing press left its mark on society. In this respect, reviewing the nature of Elizabethan military books and the interests of the reading public helps us understand why the particular relationship between print and Elizabethan military culture was so significant.

So it is important that we reconsider Maurice J. D. Cockle's *A Bibliography of Military Books up to 1642* which demonstrates a sure indication of popular interest in their subject. Indeed, Cockle's *Bibliography* is invaluable to prove that military subjects were at the

---

[7] For example, studies such as Paul Jorgensen's *Shakespeare's Military World* (19 56), Nick de Somogyi's *Shakespeare's Theatre of War* (1998) and Nina Taunton's *1590s Drama and Militarism* (2001) examine the issues concerning Elizabethan dramatic representations of military subjects.

[8] Breight, *Surveillance, Militarism and Drama in the Elizabethan Era*; Ide, "Tamburlaine's Prophetic Oratory and Protestant Militarism in the 1580s", pp. 215-36.

[9] Fortescue, *A History of the British Army,* p. 130.

centre of the life of the age.[10] According to Cockle's *Bibliography*, both English translations of ancient and modern military books and new English military books, including treatises, pamphlets and monographs of military subjects were produced at an unprecedented rate during Elizabeth's reign. For example, Cockle estimates that between 1489 and 1642 about two-hundred military books were printed in England. Of these two-hundred books, fifty-one (over twenty-five percent) were printed between the years 1585 and 1603. This assertion reveals that military subject books held a strong place in Elizabethan culture.

However, one may say that despite such an apparent increase in the number of publication of military books, the figures that Cockle's *Bibliography* indicates are at best two or three percent of printers' total output.[11] Needless to say, the proportion of military books alone is too small to suggest that military culture substantially developed in this period. But if we include histories, news pamphlets and broadside ballads featuring military affairs either by reporting specific engagements or serving pro-military propaganda, we will see that the number of published military books considerably increased. Moreover, given that many of them went on to two, three, or even more editions, it can be said that militaristic oriented books served to satisfy both Elizabethan readers and printers.[12]

For Cockle, a military book is a specialised book devoted to military affairs to a significant degree, such as the art of war, fortification, artillery and military medicine. But in my consideration, a military book is not necessarily a highly specialised book, aiming at the specialised reader, because a military book can also be a mixture of religion, politics, history, science and current news. For example, a search on *Early English Books Online (EEBO)* between the years 1558 and 1603 using "military" as a subject keyword reveals sixty records including contemporary military, mathematical, medical treatises, news pamphlets, sermons and martial laws. Interestingly, writers of those books include not only contemporary soldiers, but also contemporary poets, historians, mathematicians, prose-fiction writers and preachers. Given such the wide range of authors, my emphasis on military books can therefore go beyond the common belief

---

[10] Cockle, *Bibliography of Military Books up to 1642*.

[11] Barnard and McKenzie, *The Cambridge History of the Book in Britain*, Vol. IV 1557-1695, "Appendix 1: Statistical tables", pp. 779-82. See also Bennett, *English Books and Readers 1558 to 1603*.

[12] There were multiple editions of military books during the 1570s and 1590s. See Leonard Diggies' *Stratioticos* (1579), William Bourne's *The Arte of Shooting* (1587), Machiavelli's *The Arte of Warre* (1588) and Paul Ive's *The Practice of Fortification* (1589).

that a military book was a specialised book for a soldier. With my speculation in mind, I drew up a basic list of military books from Cockle's *Bibliography* and developed it by perusing *The Short-Title Catalogue*. Although in many cases, the short title did not necessarily match its content, histories, scientific treatises, printed sermons, ballads, pamphlets and prose-fictions could be seriously regarded as Elizabethan military books.

III

In Elizabethan military books which covered every conceivable aspect of war, knowledge of the classics were essential, because the study of military books lay in study of the classics; these classics were philosophy, education, medicine and, more than anything else, ancient histories. It was particularly the military activities of the ancient Romans and Greeks which was given light by English translators and military writers. For example, at a time when Henry VIII was at war with France, Sir Anthony Cope translated Livy's account of the campaigns of Hannibal and Scipio and dedicated it to King Henry by saying "in the readyng thereof, men also may learne both to doe displeasure to their enemies, and to auoyde the crafty and daungerous baites, which shall be layde for them".[13] Similarly, in the dedication of *The Historie of Quintus Curcius* John Brend recommended his history to the Duke of Northumberland, Marshal of England by emphasising that Alexander the Great was brought up reading history and slept with Homer under his pillow.[14]

In a similar fashion, the Roman world and its military values became a focal point not only in Elizabethan political and cultural life, but also in military life. As C. H. Conley suggests in his *The First English Translators of the Classics,* the leading persons in Elizabeth's court, expecting possible attacks by Scotland and Spain, and seeing growing threats from the counter-Reformation efforts within and without the realm, took deliberate efforts to produce the translations of the classics in order to strengthen the government.[15] As part of these efforts, certain books on the art of war intending to reform and reorganise Elizabeth's army were published. Among them were William Barker's translations of *Chronicle of the Romanes Warres* (1578) and *Bookes of Xenophon* (1552; 1567),

---

[13] Cope, trans. *The historie of two the moste noble captaines of the worlde, Anniball and Scipio.*

[14] Brend, trans. *The historie of Quintus Curtius.* It was reprinted eight times between years 1553 and 1613.

[15] Conley, *The First English Translators of the Classics,* pp. 34-45.

Onosander's *Of the Generall Captaine* (1563), Machiavelli's *The Arte of Warre* (1560), Arthur Golding's translation of *Commentaries of Julius Caesar* (1565), and John Sadler's translation of *Vegetius* (1572).[16] In this respect, it is interesting to note that during the sixteenth century four English translations of Caesar's *Commentaries* were published, three of these during the latter part of Elizabeth reign. As for its multiple editions, one may say that an interest in Caesar's writing was driven by Elizabethans' interest in matters of war. Of course, like other classical texts, Caesar's own writings were read in English schools during the Renaissance because of its rhetorical values.[17] But any Elizabethan who read John Saddler's *Vegetius* also knew that Caesar's *Commentaries* was praised by Vegetius because reading *Caesar* was a "farre better and shorter ways to attaine to the name of a worthy and perfect Captaine to ioyne experience vnto knowledge, then to get knowledge by experience".[18] It is likely then that many Elizabethans looked upon English translations of Caesar's *Commentaries* by Arthur Golding or by Sir Clement Edmond not as a history, but as an exposition upon the art of war, as Edmond commended his translation of *Caesar* to the readers by saying "Reading and discourse are requisite to make a souldier perfect in the Arte militarie, how great soever his knowledge may be which long experience and much practise in Armes hath gained".[19]

To establish how important the reading of ancient history as military history was to the Elizabethans as another avenue for politics and war, it is worth examining a passage from Sir Henry Wotton's commonplace book:

> In reading a history, a soldier should draw the platform of battles he meets with, plant the squadrons and order the whole frame as he finds it written, so he shall print it firmly in his mind and apt his mind for actions. A politique should find the characters of the personage and apply them to some of the Court he lives in, which will likewise confirm his memory and give scope and matter for conjecture and invention.[20]

It is also worth pointing out that a contemporary soldier, Sir John Smythe, followed exactly what Wotton emphasised; he read history, studied classical histories of Thucydides, Alexander the Great, Livy, Caesar, Tacitus and so on, for nurturing art and science of military:

---

[16] Conley 46.

[17] Baldwin, *William Shakespeare's Small Latine & Lesse Greeke*, 2: 565.

[18] Vegetius, *The Four Bookes of Flauius Vegetius*, Preface.

[19] Edmond, *Observations, Upon the Five Bookes of Caesars Commentaries,* Book 1.

[20] Smith, *The Life and Letters of Sir Henry Wotton,* 2: 494.

I even from my very tender years have delighted to hear histories read that
did treat of actions and deeds of arms, and since I came to years of some
discretion and that by my father's rank I was brought up to school and
brought with time to understand the Latin tongue somewhat indifferently, I
did always delight and procure my tutors as much as I could to read unto
me the commentaries of Julius Caesar and Sallust and other such books.
And after that I came from school and went to the university [...] I gave my
selfe to the reading of many other histories and books treating of matter of
war and sciences tending to the same.[21]

The Elizabethans' particular interest in reading history was virtually
coincident with the emergence of the printing of English history. There is
no question that history served the contemporary in various ways: as the
fulfilment of God's will, the library of ancient wisdom or knowledge, the
calendar of time, the alternative to memory and, more importantly, stories
of military actions. But just as Greek and Roman histories were records of
actions and concerns about councils, battles, invasions and civil wars, so
the same could be said about English chronicles. For example, Hall's
Union concentrates on the century of civil wars, and Holinshed's
Chronicles deals with the centuries of war and peace of three kingdoms as
its main subject, highlighted with various woodcut scenes of battle.[22] In
this respect, it is not surprising to see that one historian added Hall's and
Holinshed's works to the list of Tudor military history sources.[23]

By the help of numerous printed editions, these ancient and English
histories of civil wars, or war and peace soon became an obsessive theme
for contemporary popular writers including Shakespeare. As Andrew Gurr
notes, from Marlowe's Tamburlaine or Shakespeare's warlike Harry, the
masculine affairs of war and military history pervade the repertories of the
period.[24] It is almost certain that numerous editions and translations of the
classical texts were read as military books by Elizabethans as

---

[21] Lansdowne MS 54, 77, November 15. I quoted the passage from the letter Sir
John Smythe sent to Lord Burghley in 1587, see also Smythe, *Certain Discourses
Military*, ed. J. R. Hale, Introduction, xv; pp. 36-8. Smythe recommended several
books mainly ancient histories to future soldier-students for learning the basics of
military by reading.

[22] Holinshed, *The firste volume of the Chronicles of England, Scotland, and
Ireland* (1577). Holinshed anachronistically used the woodcuts of the sixteenth
century battle scene in the history of ancient England.

[23] Read, *Bibliography of British History: Tudor Period, 1495-160*, 219-27. On the
other hand, Read suggests that Hall and Holinshed are the most useful sources of
Tudor military histories.

[24] Gurr, *Playgoing in Shakespeare's London*, p. 161.

Shakespeare's Welsh captain Fluellen might have read. In other words, in the same way as printed editions of Plutarch's histories, so too did Hall's and Holinshed's provide far wider exposure of the histories to popular writers who turned to them for materials to feed the public's interests; the classics became commodities for those who might have wished to be perfect soldiers. This particular relationship between history and military, namely the presence of readers and audiences who wanted to consume them, explains why the historical books were worth printing.

IV

The classical texts and early modern history seem the only means to access military experience in an age without newspapers of modern conception. However, contemporary printing culture began to produce occasional news pamphlets and broadsides ballads responding to the reading public who were hungry for news of foreign warfare. More than anything else, these news pamphlets played their part as primary sources for reporting the campaigns in France and the Low Countries between 1589 and 1604.[25] As D. C. Collins' *A Handlist of News Pamphlets* shows, war was the theme of the majority of the pamphlets that provide a first-hand picture of war under Elizabethan conditions. For example, *A journal of or briefe report of the late seruice in Britaign* (1591) offers an account of the English expedition troops to the Elizabethans who were anxious for news of their fighting forces in France:

> Without the succour sent hither by the Queene of England, Brittaigne had beene greatly in danger…who in that respect is greatly bound vnto her Majesty. It is a very faire and galland troupe of men, and are commanded by a braue Captain Generall Norreis, a man very tractable, and with whom we are well fitted in disposition.[26]

Elsewhere, *A true discourse of the most horrible and barbarous murthers and massacres committed by the troupes of the Duke of Sauoye* (1590) provides a long list of murder and rape with sensitive detail as other war pamphlets of this time frequently did:

> *James Messier* being striken ouer his belly, so that his intralles did issue forth, dyed in few days after. The wife of the said Messier was so sore beaten, that she can neuer be her owne woman again. *Peter Riondet*, killed

---

[25] Collins, *A Handlist of News Pamphlets 1590-1610*, p. ix.

[26] Collins, p. xxxix.

as he came out of his bed although he was twentie years olde, His wife is
sore hurt, and is like hardly to recouer it. Both her daughters defloured, and
the one so hurt that the intrals come forth of her body, fifteene and
eighteene years of age.[27]

Furthermore, the news pamphlets caught readers' attention with
interesting descriptions of the conditions of war:

a munition of loaf which is of very black bread, and is about the bigness of
one of our halfpenny loaves is there sold in [the] camp for two shillings
and sixpence [and Parisians] are in wofull case for want of foode. They are
enforced to eate horses, Asses, Dogges, Cattes, Rattes, Mice, and other
filthe and unaccustomed things for their sustenance [...] through
feeblenesse and want of victuals, they fall downe dead in the streets and in
their houses.[28]

Given their exposure to such descriptions of horror of war, London
citizens easily fell into panic struck upon "news (yet false) that the
Spaniards were landed in the Isle of Wright, which bred such a fear and
consternation in this town [...] with such a cry of women, chaining of
streets and shutting of the gates".[29]

  Similarly, public interest in military affairs on the course of war was
also mirrored on the publication of ballads. But ballads, unlike news
pamphlets, favoured imagination over accuracy when dealing with their
subject. However, despite their fictional and dramatic qualities, the
ballads would have made a lasting impression on their readers. For
example, one of Thomas Deloney's propagandic ballads, published about
the time of the Spanish Armada reports Queen Elizabeth's visit to the
camp at Tilbury, recounts the queen's rousing speech as follows:

[T]hen bespake our noble Queene,
my loving friends and countriemen:
I hope this day the worst is seene,
that in out wars ye shall sustaine.
But if our enemie doe assaile you,
neuer let your stomackes faile you.
For in the midst of all your troupe,
we our selues will be in place:
To be your ioy, your guide and comfort,

---

[27] Collins, p. xix.
[28] Collins, p. lxi; p. xvi.
[29] McClure, ed. *The Letters of John Chamberlain*, 1: 78.

euen before our enemies face.[30]

Almost certainly Deloney's narrative might have moved down to the years between the 1620s and 1630s, when Elizabeth's armour and speech became an icon of national unity symbolising militant Protestantism [31] Elsewhere, Deloney, using jingoistic and xenophobic language, attempted to unify Englishmen in a defence against the Spanish soldiers:

> Before our deathes [the Spaniards] did deuise
> to whip vs first their fill.
> And for that purpose had prepared
> Of whips such wondrous store,
> So strangely made...
> That euery strole might teare the flesh
> they layd on with the same,
> And pluck the spreading sinews from
> the hardned bloudie bone...
> And set the Ladies great with childe
> vpright against tree,
> And shoot them through with pearching darts,
> such would their practise bee.[32]

Knowing the fictional nature of these ballads, there were always questions on the trustworthiness of these stories. Nevertheless, the war images projected by popular literature contributed considerably to making a collective war experience in late Elizabethan England, suggesting that the prevailing feeling of the time was physically and emotionally militaristic.

V

In a very turbulent period of Elizabeth's reign Elizabethans were attracted by stories of wars; however, as seen from the above examples, these stories were told not only by military treatises, but also various literary genres like histories, news pamphlets and ballads. Therefore, considering that the Elizabethans' military experience was thus shaped by reading a variety of books including ancient histories, mathematics, martial laws, news pamphlet and ballads, I would add these to the list of Elizabethan military books. Furthermore, given that the Elizabethans' ideal curriculum

---

[30] Deloney, *The Works of Thomas Deloney*, pp. 477-8.
[31] Frye, "The Myth of Elizabeth at Tilbury", p. 95.
[32] *The Works of Thomas Deloney* pp. 479-81.

of military education consisted of handling weapons, gymnastics, ancient and modern history, mathematics, languages, art of war and other sciences, a major selection of these books can also be considered military books.[33] In this respect, if we add other literary genres touching military subjects to the list of Elizabethan military books, we see the proportion of military books of the late sixteenth century rises to about twenty per cent of total annual output. For example, in the extraordinary year of the Spanish Armada (1588), out of 220 printed books, about forty publications could be classified as military books (18%). Among them were military treatises like Niccolò Tartaglia's *Arte of Shooting*, military medical treatises like William Clowes' *A prooued practise for all young chirurgians*, Militant Protestant sermons like *A short apologie for Christian Souldiours* and patriotic ballads like *An exhortation to all English subjects, to join for the defence of Queene Elizabeth*. Furthermore, in the same year, Whitehorne's *Certain Waies for the orderyng of Souldiers*, and Machiavelli's *The Arte of Warre* were reprinted in third editions.[34] Considering that a great number of Elizabethan books were printed only once or twice, these editions indicate that they had been circulated widely as popular works, and also suggest that there was a considerable public interest in military affairs, especially at a time when religious literature, the most popular literature of the time, including the bible, prayer books and printed sermons, held approximately thirty per cent of the total output. The proportion of military books, which amounted to the twenty percent of total output, raises their profile to the second largest category, emphasising their high significance.[35] Therefore, when the total output of military books during the last years of Elizabeth's reign is reconsidered in this way, it can be argued that Elizabethan military culture, largely shaped by the printing press, might have been one of the most conspicuous features of the Elizabethan cultural terrain.

---

[33] Hale, "The Military Education of the Officer Class", pp. 237-42; Gilbert, *Queene Elizabethes Academy*.

[34] In *STC*, Peter Whitehorne's *Certain Waie* was identified with Machiavelli's *Arte of Warre*. See Appendix I. Table 3. Registered Books in 1588.

[35] Hunt, "Books and Readers, 1588-1590", pp. 1-3; Bennet, *Book and Readers 1558 to 1603*, pp. 112-3.

Works Cited

Anon. *An exhortation to all English subjects, to join for the defence of Queene Elizabeth.* 1588.

Bacon, Francis. *The Novum Organon or A True Guide to the Interpretation of Nature.* Trans. G. W. Kitchin. Oxford: Oxford UP, 1855.

Baldwin, William. *William Shakespeare's Small Latine & Lesse Greeke.* 2 vols. Urbana: University of Illinois Press, 1944.

Barnard, J. and D. F. McKenzie. Eds. *The Cambridge History of the Book in Britain,* Vol. IV 1557-1695. Cambridge: Cambridge UP, 2002.

Bennett, H. S. *English Books and Readers 1558 to 1603.* Cambridge: Cambridge UP, 1965.

Bourne, William.*The Arte of Shooting.* 1587.

Boynton, Lindsay. *The Elizabethan Militia.* Newton Abbot: David & Charles, 1967.

Breight, Curtis C. *Surveillance, Militarism and Drama in the Elizabethan Era.* London: Macmillan, 1996.

Brend, John. Trans. *The historie of Quintus Curtius.* 1553.

Camden, William. *Remains Concerning Britain.* London, 1870.

Clowes, William. *A prooued practise for all young chirurgians.* 1588.

Cockle, Maurice J. D. *A Bibliography of Military Books up to 1642.* London: The Holland Press, 1957.

Collins, D. C. *A Handlist of News Pamphlets 1590-1610.* London: Southwest Essex Technical College, 1943.

Conley, C. H. *The First English Translators of the Classics.* Port Washington: Kennikat Press, 1967.

Cope, Sir Anthony. Trans. *The historie of two the moste noble captaines of the worlde, Anniball and Scipio.* 1544.

Cruickshank, C. G. *Elizabeth's Army.* Oxford: Clarendon, 1966.

Deloney, Thomas. *The Works of Thomas Deloney,* ed. Francis Oscar Mann. Oxford: The Clarendon Press, 1912.

Diggies, Leonard. *Stratioticos.* 1579.

Edmond, Sir Clement. *Observations, Upon the Five Bookes of Caesars Commentaries.* 1600.

Eisenstein, Elizabeth L. *The Printing Press an Agent of Change.* Cambridge: Cambridge UP, 1980.

Fortescue, J. W. *A History of the British Army.* London: Macmillan and Co., Limited, 1910.

Frye, Susan. "The Myth of Elizabeth at Tilbury." *Sixteenth Century Journal,* 23: 1 (1992); 95-114.

Garrard, William. *The Arte of Warre.* 1591.

Gilbert, Sir Humphrey. *Queene Elizabethes Academy.* Ed. F. J. Furnivall. London, 1869.

Gurr, Andrew. *Playgoing in Shakespeare's London.* Cambridge: Cambridge UP, 1996.

Hale, J. R. *Renaissance War Studies.* London: The Hambledon Press, 1983.

—. *War and Society in Renaissance Europe 1450-1620.* London: Fontana, 1985.

Holinshed, Raphael. *The firste volume of the Chronicles of England, Scotland, and Ireland.* 1577.

Hunt, Betty Chandler. *Books and Readers, 1588-1590.* Diss. Univ. of Birmingham, 1964.

Ide, Arata. "Tamburlaine's Prophetic Oratory and Protestant Militarism in the 1580s". In *Hot Questrists after the English Renaissance: Essays on Shakespeare and His Contemporaries*, ed. by Yasunari Takahashi. New York: AMS Press, 2000, 215-36.

Ive, Paul. *The Practice of Fortification.* 1589.

Languet, Hubert. *A Short Apologie for Christian Souldiours.* 1588.

Machiavelli, Niccolò. *The Arte of Warre.* 1560; 1588.

McClure, Norman E. Ed. *The Letters of John Chamberlain.* 2 vols. Philadelphia: The American Philosophical Society, 1939.

Parker, Geoffrey. *The Military Revolution: Military Innovation and the Rise of the West 1500-1800.* Cambridge: Cambridge UP, 1999.

Read, Conyers. *Bibliography of British History: Tudor Period, 1495-1603.* Oxford: The Clarendon Press, 1933.

Shakespeare, William. *Henry IV, Part I.* Ed. David Bevington. Oxford: Oxford UP, 1998.

Smith, L. P. *The Life and Letters of Sir Henry Wotton.* Oxford, 1907.

Smythe, Sir John. *Certain Discourses Military.* Ed. J. R. Hale. Ithaca: New York, 1964.

Spaulding, Thomas M. "Elizabethan Military Books". *Joseph Quincy Adams Memorial Studies.* Eds. James G. McManaway and et al. Washington: The Folger Shakespeare Library, 1948; 495-507.

Taraglia, Niccolò. *Arte of Shooting.* 1588.

Vegetius, Flavius R. *The Four Bookes of Flauius Vegetius,* 1572.

Whitehorne, Peter. *Certain Waies for the orderyng of Souldiers.* 1562; 1588.

CHAPTER FIVE

ACTORS, AUDIENCES AND AUTHORS: THE COMPETITION FOR CONTROL IN BROME'S *THE ANTIPODES*

AUDREY BIRKETT

Throughout the 1630s the commercial theatre was increasingly mired in economic, social, and political crises. The professional theatre was under strain toward the end of the Caroline era as opposition increased both from within the dramatic community and from different factions in the wider society. The competition for audience favour amongst the different commercial theatres led to somewhat hostile relations and derogatory slander between the playhouses. The citizen theatres like the Red Bull received the harshest treatment, whilst playwrights writing for the prestigious Blackfriars decried all other theatres as being too crude and vulgar for respectable patrons.[1] Not only did professional playwrights face opposition from their professional peers, but they also had to defend themselves against the slights of the amateur courtier poets who were writing for the commercial stage. The Caroline audiences seemed to desire the plays that more closely resembled those staged at court that the amateur writers were producing rather than those comedies that were more in the vein of the Elizabethan and Jacobean plays that had been staged at the public theatres.[2] The pressure on the professional playwrights was further compounded by sanitation concerns. Plague closures threatened to put an end to the public theatrical institution at the same time the Puritan faction was mounting opposition toward the ribaldry they associated with

---

[1] See Gurr, *The Shakespearean Stage*, pp. 201-203. Gurr discusses the hostility that is displayed by various playwrights of the Caroline era who use the theatrical affiliation to criticise their peers.

[2] See Neill, "'Wits Most Accomplished Senate': The Audience of Caroline Private Theatres", pp. 341-360 and Gurr, *The Shakespearean Stage*, pp. 199-215.

the London playhouses. Publication was also becoming an attractive
option for playwrights who had not relinquished the rights to their plays
after selling them to companies to be staged. Within this context, as I will
show, Richard Brome's *The Antipodes* directly addresses all of these
threats in turn. Brome criticises one playing company, whilst praising
another. He turns the scrutiny of the Puritans and the courtiers back on
themselves. He diminishes the threats posed by the plague and encourages
the audiences to return to the theatres. He also portrays those in the courtly
circle as foolish and insincere. In a play that's based on opposites and
reversals, Brome highlights and stresses the threats to the real-life London
theatrical society by demonstrating what the alternatives may be.

When Brome originally wrote *The Antipodes* he intended it not for the
players of Salisbury Court, but for The King and Queen's Young
Company performing at William Beeston's Cockpit. There had been
contractual disputes between Brome and Salisbury Court leading up to
Brome's writing of the play. He was obliged to write three plays a year for
the company and could not publish any of the plays that he had written for
them of his own accord.[3] However, when the theatres closed in 1636,
Salisbury Court suspended Brome's wages forcing him to seek an
alternative income at the Cockpit. The play was never staged at Beeston's
theatre, however but was instead bought back by Salisbury Court and
staged in 1638 after the theatres had reopened. Brome seemed dissatisfied
with the performance and thus initiated the printing of the play in 1640,
thereby again breaking the terms of his contract with Salisbury Court.
Brome's post-script in the published version suggests that his original play
was altered slightly for the 1638 performance to fit time constraints and
possibly to avoid the controversy Brome had inserted into the drama
against Salisbury Court.[4] Brome seems to have found fault with the
staging and made amends to what was removed, calling attention to the
fact that his words had been tampered with by the theatrical company. The
1640 printed version seems to have been written and re-edited by Brome
himself and firmly declares that he holds the authority over the play.
Through the different versions, the author, the actors, and the theatre
manager leave a distinct mark on the play which brings into question who
holds final authority over a play. Brome asserted his ownership when he
gave it to Beeston for performance at the Cockpit. However, Beeston then

---

[3] See Steggle, *Richard Brome: Place and Politics on the Caroline Stage*, pp. 105-
118. The contract clause was reinforced by the addendum that he could not initiate
the publication of any of the plays that he wrote for the Salisbury Court, regardless
of whether or not they were staged.
[4] Brome, *The Antipodes*, 1.1.1-9.

demonstrated his authority over the play by getting it printed.[5] The vigorous reclaiming of the play from Beeston's Cockpit by Salisbury Court suggests the theatrical company was eager to establish firm control over the play and thus over Brome himself who was legally contracted to the theatre. Finally, the publication of the play, complete with post-scripts and amendments, restored the power of authority back to Brome.

Widely considered a playwright for the stage and a defender of the commercial theatre, Brome adopted, at times, a slightly detached attitude toward both the stage and the wider institution of the commercial theatre in *The Antipodes*. The very insistence on writing it for the Cockpit, a stage with which he was not affiliated and defying the contractual obligations he was under, detracts from the idea that Brome had cultivated throughout his career, the belief the stage came first, even above the playwright. He had spent a career criticising the courtier poets who tended to write for the most select of theatres and yet when writing *The Antipodes*, Brome decidedly set it to be staged in a theatre that was foreign to him. His further decision to publish the play also contradicts the reputation he had established as a writer for the stage. Only three of his plays were printed during his lifetime, despite the fact that more were entered into the Stationers' Register prior to the publication of *The Antipodes*.[6] Despite his feigned aversion to publication, those plays that went to press in his lifetime seem to have been initiated by the dramatist himself, and, even more surprising, conformed to the expectations of publication, including fawning commendations from peers and sycophantic dedications to gentlemen patrons. However, only *The Antipodes* and *The Sparagus*

---

[5] Steggle, *Richard Brome*, p. 118. Brome's contract with Salisbury Court stipulated that he could not print the plays that he wrote for the company without consent from them. Brome's falling out with the company led him to join Beeston's company at the Cockpit in 1639, a year before *The Antipodes* was printed. It is unlikely that the company at Salisbury Court would initiate the printing of the play with the changes and additions that are included in the published version and which effectively blame and chastise the company for ruining Brome's original intentions. It makes sense that Brome himself initiated the printing, thereby breaking the terms of his original contract, in order to restore his original message and stress his intent.

[6] See Steggle, *Richard Brome*, pp. 156-157. On 4 August 1640, Brome entered six plays into the Stationers' Register for publication. Those being *Chistianetta*, *The Jewish Gentleman*, *A New Academy* or *Exchange*, *The Love Sick Court*, *The Covent Garden Weeded*, and *The English Moore*. The plays were never printed, however, and subsequently, two of these plays have been lost. The remainder of Brome's plays, including four of the six he initiated the printing of in 1640 would not be published until after his death in 1652.

Garden were printed in 1640 and the fact that several of the others never reached the printer shows hesitancy toward publication. Brome did initiate the printing of several more plays in 1640 after his chief rival William Davenant took control over the Cockpit when Beeston was suspended for allowing controversial plays to appear on his stage. It would appear as though the move was simply a reaction to the courtier writers' threat against the commercial theatre and not a desire on Brome's part to see his name in print.[7] Yet the 1640 publication of *The Antipodes* is a reassertion of authorial rights and a bold proclamation of authority against the commercial theatre.

The Antipodes is about the therapeutic nature of the theatre and its ability to restore the natural order. The primary focus is on Peregrine, a young man who has gone mad from reading too many travel narratives and thus has lost touch with reality. To combat his son's illness, the gentleman Joyless hires a doctor to cure Peregrine's delusions. The doctor arranges an elaborate play whereby Peregrine can act out his dreams of travelling and thus purge the fantastic desire. It is at the Lord Letoy's private theatre that the spectacle is staged and Peregrine travels to the Antipodes – a world that mirrors his own. By showing Peregrine the opposite of what he's accustomed to, the doctor creates an environment that is both remarkably similar and exceptionally alien to the patient, thereby demonstrating the benefits of the real society he has been alienated from. Through the staging of the farce, Peregrine's senses are restored and at the same time Joyless's martial problems with his young, beautiful wife, Diana, are mended, and long-lost families are reconciled. The play ends with a return to the normal, "real" world where all are restored to their natural places and natural states, but it is only thanks to Letoy's fictional "The Antipodes" that such a restoration occurs. Brome champions the commercial theatre as a place of therapy and escape, allowing the pressures from the "real" world to be alleviated. Brome treated the theatre as a place for catharsis and therapy and through comedy he could combat "melancholy, his age's pervasive disease".[8] Nevertheless, just as Peregrine, Joyless, and Diana must return to their everyday lives, so to are

---

[7] See Freehafer, "Brome, Suckling, and Davenant's Theatre Project of 1639", pp. 367-383. It seems as though Davenant stopped Brome's plays from being printed at the Cockpit and thus Brome again had to look to alternate methods to get his plays out into the public sphere, this time being publication. Brome's initiating the printing of six plays seems to have been a reaction to Davenant's placement at the Cockpit, rather than his desire to further his name and reputation through print.

[8] Nania, "Richard Brome" in *Dictionary of Literary Biography*, p. 27.

the curative effects of the theatre temporary as a return to normality is what is expected and inevitable.

The parallels between the plot of the play and its staging (both intended and probable) could not have been lost on Brome who was, by 1636, one of the premier professional playwrights. Although he maintained a prominent position in the professional theatre, writing *The Antipodes* for an alternative commercial stage mirrors the outline of the play as the characters seemingly travel to a place that is very like their home, but different, and at times more accommodating and agreeable. David Stevens contends that the private commercial theatres were very similar which allowed plays to be interchangeable amongst the different stages.[9] With the similarities between the different, up-scale commercial theatres being so prevalent, it became a question of what company was situated in a particular theatre, and to Brome, what manager was in charge. Beeston was a widely respected and revered theatre manager and moreover, he and Brome seemed to have a personal, friendly relationship.[10] The more amenable conditions at the Cockpit suggested Brome could have exercised more creative control over the production.

Brome's growing anger and disillusionment toward the professional theatre, and more specifically toward Salisbury Court, is seen through what he included in the ancillary material of the published version. The dedication to William Seymour, the Earl of Hertford displays a need, on Brome's behalf, for publication.

> If the publicke view of the world entertain it with no lesse welcome, then that private one of the Stage already has given it, I shall be glad the World owes you the Thankes: if it meet with too severe Construction, I hope your Protection. What hazards soever it shall justle with, my desires are it may pleasure your Lordship in the perusal, which is the only ambition he is conscious of, who is My Lord, Your Honour's humble devoted: Richard Brome.[11]

---

[9] Stevens, "The Staging of Plays at the Salisbury Court Theatre, 1630-1642", pp. 522-523.

[10] Eades Bentley, *The Jacobean and Caroline Stage*, Vol. VI, "Theatres", pp. 71-72. Bentley contends that "Beeston as a manager, producer, and coach at the Phoenix must have been a significant influence in the drama of late Caroline London."

[11] Brome, "To the Right Honourable William Earle of Hertford, &c" in *The Antipodes*.

Brome's terming of the stage as "private" and his belief in the "publicke"
domain of the printed book runs contrary to the previous notions he had
issued in plays and prologues.[12] The stage had always been the place for a
play and it was important that anyone and everyone had access to drama in
performance. Furthermore, the price of books and the relatively low level
of literacy meant that only certain (often higher class) patrons could
purchase and consume printed play texts.[13] Because the play had been
staged at Salisbury Court, Brome could be criticising the exclusivity of the
theatre as being too "private" for what he had written. However, the
Cockpit was not an open, public theatre inviting all and sundry, but rather
it enjoyed a very privileged clientele.[14] His dedication to the "Earle of
Hertford, &c" further suggests that Brome was opening the play up to a
wider audience than it had previously been available to, and that the
audience is mixed and varied as is the "&c". His primary dedicatee,
however, is Hertford, a well respected and well connected gentleman.[15]
His further declaration that he hopes the play receives Hertford's
"Protection" suggests a boastful assertion that it is above his dedicatee's
reproach, a contrast to the attitude Brome has adopted in the past where he
begged audiences for a kind reception. This assertion makes Brome sound
more like the courtier dramatists that he opposed, especially when he
declares his "only ambition" is to please Hertford and not to entertain the
audience, which had previously been his primary aim. He finally declares
himself Hertford's "humble" devotee, which again conflicted with
Brome's past declarations of subservience to the commercial theatre
audiences. The dedication gave authority to Hertford over the play, in the
process taking it away from the theatre where it had previously been
known. Brome's giving it to Hertford is also an attempt to re-establish his
own authority over *The Antipodes*. It is now his to give away rather than

---

[12] Brome, *The Sparagus Garden*, prologue and Brome, *The Antipodes*, prologue.
The Sparagus Garden, which was printed in the same year as *The Antipodes*,
displays much more antagonism toward publication. In the prologue, Brome
contends "It sayes the *Sparagus Garden*; if you looke/To feast on that, the Title
spoiles the Booke." Even the prologue to *The Antipodes* itself decries publication
as the primary means of transmission for a play when he says that "Workes, that
must ever live upon the Stage".

[13] Cressy, *Literacy and the Social Order: Reading and Writing in Tudor and Stuart
England*, specifically pp. 121-122. Cressy maps out the levels of literacy across
social borders and, not surprisingly, it is the higher classes that have a much higher
level of learning than the lower orders.

[14] Eades Bentley, *The Jacobean and Caroline Stage*, V, p. 6.

[15] See Smith, "William Seymour, first marquess of Hertford and Second Duke of
Somerset" and Brome, *The Northern Lasse* and *The Sparagus Garden*.

the possession of the "private" audiences whom had already "given it" their judgement.

The post-script that Brome added to the published version of *The Antipodes* does little to clarify Brome's attitude toward the professional theatre or demarcate the ultimate authority over the play. Whereas he seems to have given ownership to Hertford in the dedication, Brome gives possession to Beeston in the epilogue.

> You shal find in this Booke more then was presented upon the *Stage*, and left out of the *Presentation*, for superfluous length (as some of the *Players* pretended) I thoght good al should be inserted according to the allowed *Original*; and as it was, at first, intended for the *Cock-pit Stage*, I the right of my most deserving Friend Mr. *William Beeston*, unto whom it properly appertained.[16]

Brome gives authority to Beeston "unto whom [the play] properly appertained". However, as it is now in printed form and not a staged presentation, the ownership seems questionable with Brome, the literary audience, and Beeston all able to claim ownership and authority over it. Brome stresses the "Booke" is now the most important item as it contains all that he had intended for the stage. As such, it would be the reader who exerted complete control over the literature. At the same time, Brome clearly states that it is Beeston who is the controlling agent as he is the one that the play was intended for from the start. Nevertheless, Brome's switching of authority suggests that it is he who is the ultimate controller over the play and dictator of its fate. The one group that he does not allocate any form of authority to, however, is the players. He begrudges their attempts to assert authority over the play. All of this is further complicated by the manner in which the epilogue is printed. Assuming that Brome did exert control over the publication, the decision to highlight the words "Stage", "Presentation", "Players", "Original", "Cock-pit Stage", and "William Beeston" suggest close ties and a determined affiliation with the performance as opposed to the published book.[17]

Although *The Antipodes* does ultimately praise the therapeutic power of the theatre, it also exposes the complications that arise from the

---

[16] Brome, *The Antipodes*, epilogue.

[17] Jonathan Okes printed *The Antipodes* and *The Sparagus Garden* for Brome. Okes had a hand in printing many plays from some of the most prominent playwrights including Shakespeare and Jonson. As Jonson was known to have been very strict with his control over the publication of his "Workes" it is likely that Okes was not opposed to giving creative control to the authors.

competition for control between the actors, the writers, the authors, and the audiences. The owner of the small, private theatre, Letoy, controls the overall action and direction of the play-within-the-play from afar, as well as influences the response of Joyless, his captive audience. Letoy is also the author of the play and thus exerts even more influence and control over the play. In fact, the only thing he does not do is act, yet he still tries to keep a tight reign on how the action proceeds. He states that he "must looke to all", implying that every single aspect of the play is his to determine and control.[18] However, the insertion of Peregrine into the play as an unknowing actor alters the circumstances to the point that the original plot is dramatically changed and Letoy's power is diminished as the actors react to the participant. Although the outcome remains the same, Peregrine's cure, the direction in which it is realised is largely determined by Peregrine himself in his interactions with the acting Antipodeans. Whilst Letoy plays the role of both author and manager, it is the actors who ultimately drive the play as they react to Peregrine's whims and fancies. The whole play is staged for the benefit of the Joylesses who have facilitated the entire staging to have their son's health restored. Although Joyless's wishes are not always followed, his reactions, and those of his wife, determine the action and remain the driving force behind Brome's narration.

Letoy exerts his authority over the play by exerting his authority over the actors that he employs. As he owns his own private theatre, he keeps a private troupe that is on-hand at all times solely for his amusement:

> Stage-playes, and Masques, are nightly my pastimes,
> And all within my selfe. My owne men are
> My Musique, and my Actors. I keepe not
> A man or boy but is of quality:
> The worst can sing or play his part o'th' Violls,
> And act his part too in a Comedy,
> For which I lay my bravery on their backs;
> And where another Lord undoes his followers,
> I maintaine mine like Lords. And there's my bravery.[19]

Letoy claims that the actors belong to him and that they are, in fact, his "followers". His conceit highlights the abilities of the players, but more importantly shows the greatness of Letoy himself. "His" men are the best, therefore, "his" theatre is the best. His insistence that his actors are of the

---

[18] Brome, *The Antipodes*, II.ii.11.
[19] Brome, *The Antipodes*, I.v.62-70.

highest "quality" speaks to the high levels of competition amongst the theatres and the boastfulness of managers in attracting audiences with the promise of the best players. Letoy claims that he writes "all the playes my selfe" and even though he is responsible for what is staged, the confession that his "bravery" comes from the manner in which he keeps his players suggests that he realises they are the most important faction in playing. Despite Letoy's admittance of the importance of the players, he is still anxious to maintain strict control over the direction of the play. He is very dictatorial about what should be staged and how it is to be acted:

> Trouble not you your head with my conceite,
> But minde your part. Let me not see you act now,
> In your Scholasticke way, you brought to towne wi' yee.[20]

Letoy's advice to his actors sounds very much like Hamlet's advice to the travelling players who have come to Elsinore. He even suggests that his own troupe is lately come from the country and as such, do not fully understand how a play should be acted in "towne". His reference to "Scholasticke" acting methods suggests the actors could have come from a university troupe and they are therefore unaware of what is expected on the London stages. His directions to "trouble not you your head with [his] conceite" shows the tenuous balance of power that exists between himself and his actors. He tells the actors to disregard his "conceite", but then dictates to them how they should act, saying he will have it no other way in "his house". The play in his house makes him the ultimate authority to the point of deciding if and when a play is to be staged.

   In a later exchange with the actors, Letoy concedes some of the authority he has previously claimed by giving the actors license to interpret what he has written for themselves:

> Take license to your owne selfe, to adde unto
> Your parts, your owne free fancey; and sometimes
> To alter, or diminish what the writer
> With care and skill compose'd: and when you are
> To speake to your coactors in the Scene,
> You hold interloqutions with the Audients.[21]

In this speech to his actors, Letoy bestows on them the power to alter what is scripted as they see fit, trusting their abilities and their discretion. He is

---

[20] Brome, *The Antipodes*, II.ii.15-17.
[21] Brome, *The Antipodes*, II.ii.42-47.

sure to remind them of the importance of his own careful and skilful wording, but he admits that the power to convey the messages ultimately rests with the actors. Furthermore, his final command to acknowledge the "Audients" demonstrates the power that the viewers have and that ultimately the play is designed to be viewed. Therefore the spectator holds as much power as the actors and the interaction between the two is what drives the play and makes it successful, not the script. Letoy constantly grapples for control with his actors, yet he betrays his own belief in the importance of the players and the audience over the writer:

> Ile none of these, absurdities in my house.
> But words and action married so together,
> That shall strike harmony in the eares and eyes
> Of the severest, if judicious Criticks.[22]

Letoy himself seems to be the most "judicious Critick" of all and as he influences the reception of the plays to the small, intimate audiences he hosts, he controls to a degree how the play is viewed.

Letoy does all he can to control any and all aspect of the play and not just the actors, but the audience reception as well. As he is situated alongside the viewers, he is able to manipulate their responses to his ends:

> And for my Actors, they shall speake, or not speake
> As much, or more, or lesse, and when I please,
> It is my way of pleasure, and ile use it.
> So sit: They enter.[23]

The control the audience exerted over the play is very limited in both the actual *The Antipodes* and the fictional one. Letoy's order to the audience is "sit" and thereby respect the entrance of the actors, whom now command more attention and respect then the audience. The authority of Joyless and Diana is subject entirely to Letoy's will as he holds nearly complete influence over how the couple react to what's being staged for their benefit, manipulating them and their responses. Joyless several times expresses a desire to leave the theatre and Letoy's house. However, he is again and again denied and ends up something of a prisoner in Letoy's house in the final act. Byplay warns him to "take your dungeon Sir" suggesting that Letoy is not of his own free will, but also establishes his

---

[22] Brome, *The Antipodes*, II.ii. 68-70.
[23] Brome, *The Antipodes*, III.i.16-19.

subservient role to the actors as well as Letoy.[24] In fact, it is through the play that he is cured of his jealousy and therefore he is being manipulated and not acting of his own free will at all. All of this is designed, by Letoy, to reveal that Diana is his daughter and that Joyless has no cause for jealousy. Diane and Joyless are being manipulated from the very beginning of the play as they are invited under false pretences to the performance.

> Letoy: know sir, that I sent for him, and for you,
> Instructing your friend *Blaze* my instrument,
> To draw you to my Doctor with your sonne,
> Your wife I knew must follow, what my end
> Was in't shall quickely be discover'd to you[25]

Letoy's "The Antipodes" ends up being the design of Letoy himself and not the result of the Joyless's desire to cure their son. Although they believed this was why they were coming to Letoy's theatre, his ends are what brought them rather than their own needs. Even when he confesses that the audience did not act of their own free will, he still dictates the terms by which his motives will be discovered.

It is when Letoy exerts his role as the writer of the play that the most conflicted view of the playwright is seen. Letoy presses his status as the owner of the theatre (and subsequently the owner of the actors) and is more forceful in exerting that role than he is the role of the author. In fact, both Letoy and the actors are quick to denounce "the poet" and the privileged position held by the writers.

> For I am none of those Poeticke furies,
> That threats the Actors life, in a whole play,
> That addes a sillable, or takes away.[26]

He wishes the performance to be spontaneous and reactionary to the whims of the audience and the actors themselves. Although Letoy is proud that he is the author of the play, he will not refer to himself as a poet. Rather, he views poets as "furies" intent on destruction rather than on creation. He associates poetry with drama as he declares that the "poetic furies" threaten the actors. The decidedly anti-poet slant that is portrayed in "The Antipodes" is likely a reflection of Brome's disdain toward the

---

[24] Brome, *The Antipodes*, V.i.5.
[25] Brome, *The Antipodes*, V.vi.9-13.
[26] Brome, *The Antipodes*, II.i.23-25.

amateur courtly playwrights who termed themselves poets and who opposed the commercial theatre. In "The Antipodes", Letoy claims "all their Poets are Puritanes", which would seem to reconcile the two enemies who are normally so at odds with one another. However, as both the courtier dramatists and the Puritans were strong opponents of the professional stage with each faction wanting to eradicate the commercial theatre, the comparison makes the two extremes seem very much alike.

The critique of "poets" continues as Letoy scripts them to be professional and austere, characteristics Brome seems to have completely disassociated with the "poets" living and working during his own time. The poets in "The Antipodes" are industrious and professional, as opposed to their lazy, real-life counterparts:

> *Poet.*
> Yes, of all
> My severall wares, according to the rates
> Delivered unto my debitor,
>
> *Dia.*
> Wares does he say?
>
> *Let.*
> Yes, Poetry is good ware
> In the Antipodes, though there be some ill payers,
> As well as here; but Law there rights the Poets.[27]

The poets are professionals in the Antipodes, selling their "wares" for financial gains rather than reputation and acclaim as they do in the real London. Furthermore, the fact that the law protects these poets criticises the tendency to slight the professional writers in his real London. Brome's troubles with the Salisbury Court played a part in developing this critical attitude toward the slights at the professional dramatic community. He viewed himself as unprotected from the injustices that he found within the professional community and begrudged the protection that his non-professional, courtly counterparts enjoyed. It was this mentality that led Brome to write the play for Beeston. His own theatre's refusal to pay his wages during the closures suggested that the playwright was considered to be of lesser import than the actors or the managers and therefore it was unnecessary to pay him when no plays could be staged and new plays were not needed.

---

[27] Brome, *The Antipodes*, III.ii.14-20.

The sobriety exemplified by the Antipodean poets also runs contrary to the characterisations of the men who deemed themselves poets that Brome had created in so many of his other plays.[28] Letoy claims they "Are slow of tongue, but nimble with the pen", again implying that the reverse is true in the real London, that the real-life poets are boastful of their sub-standard work.[29] The poet is seen negotiating with a lawyer and in their final discussion, the poet tries to force money on the lawyer for his council. "The counsaile and the comfort you have given/Me, requires a double fee."[30] The notion of a poet paying for anything, including council is portrayed as outrageous and completely alien. There seemed to be a prevalent belief that the courtier poets did not pay for anything and in fact, ran into large debts that they then relied on their aristocratic allies to protect them from.[31] In the vision painted of the poets, both Brome and Letoy demonstrate them to be completely contrary and opposite to their real-life counterparts and whereas they are allies to professionalism in the upside down world, they are enemies in the real-life London.

While Letoy distances himself from the title of poet, suggesting that the writer is the least authoritative agent in dramatic production, the actors become more powerful as they gain more and more control over what occurs on stage. Peregrine's participation in the play means they have to act and react according to his behaviour:

> *Let.*
> I see th'event already, by the ayme
> The Doctor takes, proceed you with your play,
> And let him see it in what state he pleases.[32]

Peregrine's unknowing part as an actor gives his fellow thespians control over the production as he is the central concern of the fictitious

---

[28] Brome, *The Damoiselle*, *The City Wit*, and *The Love-Sick Court*. Brome was adamant that he was not a poet in *The Love-Sick Court* when he stressed in the prologue that "A little wit, lesse learning, no Poetry/This Play-maker dares boast: Tis his modesty". In *The Damoiselle*, he again emphasised that "he won't be calld/Author, or Poet".

[29] Brome, *The Antipodes*, III.ii.94.

[30] Brome, *The Antipodes*, III.ii.95-96.

[31] See Edmond, *Rare Sir William Davenant,* p. 27. Brome's chief rival, William Davenant, had been embroiled in a lawsuit with a tailor over the non-payment of fees, a case that was dismissed due to Davenant's courtly connections. The backlash created by this denoted fury over peer protection amongst the cavalier playwrights and poets.

[32] Brome, *The Antipodes*, III.v.41-43.

play. Despite Letoy's scripting and supposed advanced knowledge of how Peregrine will react to the events and circumstances around him, the actors cannot follow exactly what is put down for them as they are working with an active and participatory audience:

> *Let.*
> Hoyday! The rest will all be lost, we now give over
> The play, and doe all by *Extempore*,
> For your sonnes good, to sooth him into's wits.
> If you'l marre all, yon may. Come nearer cocks-combe,
> Ha you forgotten (puppy) my instructions
> Touching his subjects, and his marriage?[33]

Allowing the players to act extempore means that Letoy now holds no power over what is to happen next. He tries to maintain control by speaking harshly to Byplay in an attempt to solidify his authority. Byplay takes control of the situation when he is asked by Peregrine what is happening, effectively stripping any control away that Letoy may still have held:

> *Per.*
> What voyce was that?
>
> *Byp.*
> A voyce out of the clouds, that doth applaud
> Your highnesse welcome to your subjects loves.
>
> *Let.*
> So, now ho's in. Sit still, I must goe downe
> And set out things in order.[34]

Byplay's terming Letoy merely "a voyce out of the clouds, that doth applaud" makes him a spectator and not the controlling agent of the play. Letoy must go down to the stage and become a participating actor if he wants to regain the authority he once held over the production. As "The Antipodes" continues and the actors work extemporaneously, Letoy loses more and more control. It is only in the manipulation of the audience watching, Joyless and Diana, that he is still able to wield any influence. The actors now possess all the authority on the stage and are the only ones that can bring about the desired effect on Peregrine by interacting with

---

[33] Brome, *The Antipodes*, IV.ix.146-151.
[34] Brome, *The Antipodes*, IV.ix.153-157.

him. Letoy gives over the play to the actors entirely from the balcony where he is viewing the play along with his audience, the Joylesses. Although he desires to maintain control, he realises that his must "give over" in order for the play to continue on and its effect to be realised. Brome himself gave over both the original version and the published one to outside agents. He intended *The Antipodes* to go to Beeston, giving it over to him with the belief that it would be staged at the Cockpit rather than at Salisbury Court. However, by giving over the play, Brome, like the fictional Letoy, lost the ability to control the direction of his play. When he did reclaim control over the play, with print in 1640, the controlling party was impossible to define with the playwright, the dedicatee, the manager, and the literary audience all being able to claim authority, despite the admittance that it was intended for the stage, and therefore any and all involved in the staging of the play.

The result of the play-within-the-play is to restore social order and provide a happy outcome. What the control and authority over the action gives is plain to see, and as it is Letoy who exerts the most effort in controlling the play, it is his wishes and desires that are fulfilled at the end, but with benefit to all. The entire play of *The Antipodes*, however, proved to be much more divisive than its fictional by-play counterpart, not only in terms of the conflicts that it references, but also in terms of the way Brome portrays his affiliations as a professional writer. Throughout his career, Brome had carefully developed a reputation as a staunch defender of the professional, public theatre. He was an out-spoken opponent against the amateur courtier dramatists whom he felt threatened the traditions and inclusiveness of the commercial theatre. Yet in *The Antipodes* he conveys a muddled and often negative view of the professional theatre. The lack of cohesion and the growing opposition that centred on Brome demonstrated in the theatrical community of the 1630s seems to have left him with a bitter taste in his mouth. Whilst he never demonstrated a possessive attitude toward his plays, the events surrounding the performance and publication of *The Antipodes*, as well as the matter contained within each highlight the lack of control that was fundamental to the commercial theatrical community in the lateCaroline era.

Works Cited

Boas, Frederick S. *An Introduction to Stuart Drama*. Oxford: Oxford University Press, 1946.

Brome, Richard. *The Antipodes*. London: John Okes, 1640.

—. *The Northern Lasse*. London: August Matthes, 1632.

Cressy, David. *Literacy and the Social Order: Reading and Writing in Tudor and Stuart England*. Cambridge: Cambridge University Press, 1980.

Eades Bentley, Gerald. *The Jacobean and Caroline Stage*. Oxford: Clarendon Press, 1968.

Edmond, Mary. *Rare Sir William Davenant*. Manchester: Manchester University Press, 1987.

Freehafer, John. "Brome, Suckling, and Davenant's Theatre Project of 1639". *Texas Studies in Literature and Language: A Journal of the Humanities*, 10 (1968) 367-383.

Gurr, Andrew. *The Shakespearean Stage 1574-1642*. Cambridge: Cambridge University Press, 1992.

Nania, John S. "Richard Brome". In *Dictionary of Literary Biography*, Vol. 58, ed. by Fredson Bowers. Detroit.

Neill, Michael "'Wits Most Accomplished Senate': The Audience of Caroline Private Theatres". *Studies in English Literature, 1500-1900* Vol. 18, No. 2 (1978), 341-360.

Smith, David L. "William Seymour, first marquess of Hertford and Second Duke of Somerset". In *Oxford Dictionary of National Biography*. Oxford: Oxford University Press, 2004.

Steggle, Matthew. *Richard Brome: Place and Politics on the Caroline Stage*. Manchester: Manchester University Press, 2004.

Stevens, David. "The Staging of Plays at the Salisbury Court Theatre, 1630-1642". *Theatre Journal*, Vol. 31, 4 (1979), 511-525.

CHAPTER SIX

SHAKESPEARE'S *KING RICHARD III*: THE PERVERTED MACHIAVEL

CONNY LODER

With this article I want to challenge the notion that Shakespeare's character Richard III is Machiavelli's ideal prince, portrayed in his *Principe*. In fact, what Shakespeare achieves in Richard is the perversion of Machiavelli's ideal prince. To support this argument, it is important to look at the character Richard as part of the *Henry VI* plays and *Richard III* because only then can one grasp Richard's complex identity.

Due to the complexity of source material and various cultural interpretations throughout the last century,[1] Shakespeare's character Richard III has undergone three vastly differing interpretations: as an element of a player in the retribution scheme within the Tudor Myth, as a vice-figure and as a ruthless Machiavel. Initially I will briefly outline these interpretation modes.

E. M. W. Tillyard, the most prominent adherent to the critical theory of the Tudor myth, argues for a pro-Providential interpretation of Richard. In the fashion of pre-New Historicism and Cultural Materialism, Tillyard denies any influence from controversial and non-conformist Elizabethan and Renaissance writings such as Machiavelli.[2] In Tillyard's eyes, Shakespeare's history plays' sole function is to glorify England's recent past, thus reducing Richard to an orthodox means of re-establishing moral and divine order on earth, previously upset by Bullingbrook.[3] In the mood of the Old Testament, a vengeful God therefore employs Richard as a tool, so Lily Campbell tells us, and allows him to commit crimes, which are "sins against the moral order" as they appear to be "moral rather than

---

[1] See Schieder, "Shakespeare and Machiavelli", *Archiv für Kulturgeschichte,* Vol. 33, 131-173.
[2] See Tillyard, *The Elizabethan World Picture*, p. 17
[3] See Tillyard, *Shakespeare's History Plays*, p. 199.

political sins" and necessarily anticipate Richard's own fall in the
retribution scheme.[4]

Phyllis Rackin agrees that Richard is part of the retribution scheme,
but maintains that he is not an instrument of God. She argues that while
Richard believes that he lives "in a world governed by Machiavellian
Realpolitik", he actually lives in a world "governed by providence, a
dissonance that produces heavy dramatic irony in the scenes when Richard
gloats happily about the success of his machinations".[5] According to
Wolfang Iser, what remains is that an apparently self-willed Richard is
caught in the midst of an archaic and medieval world, ruled by dreams,
curses and prophecies, unsuccessfully trying to battle God, or in
Machiavelli's terms, Fortuna.[6] Edward Berry concurs; he believes that
Richard becomes an "unknowing victim of a scheme of retribution,"
whose pseudo-Machiavellian character is neither of consequence to
Richard's motivation, nor of consequence to the propulsion of the plot.[7]
None of the retribution explanations are convincing, since these critics fail
to see Richard as an active agent and restrict him to a puppet.

The question of vice versus Machiavel is discussed by critics under
the point of Richard's evil disposition. The vice defenders claim that
Richard has no obvious cause for his evil disposition. As far as they are
concerned, Richard's thinking is binary—while being good seems
impossible, being bad seems the only alternative—and so he informs the
audience in his first soliloquy in *Richard III*:

> And therefore, since I cannot prove a lover
> To entertain these fair well-spoken days,
> I am determined to prove a villain
> And hate the idle pleasures of these days. (I.i.28-31)

To dispel any doubt, he aligns himself explicitly to the devil: "And
seem a saint, when most I play the devil" (I.iii.335-337). Admittedly, this
self-depiction recalls the same determination by which Iago destroys
Othello's happiness. Hence it is understandable why Graham Holderness
sees in Richard someone who, due to exclusion from court life and his
disgust of harmony, creates for himself an "elegy for the loss of a heroic

---

[4] Campbell, *Shakespeare's Histories. Mirrors of Elizabethan Policy,* pp. 317-318;
p. 310.
[5] Rackin, *Stages of History. Shakespeare's English Chronicles,* p. 63.
[6] See Iser, *Staging Politics. The Lasting Impact on Shakespeare's Histories,* pp.
46-48.
[7] Berry, *Patterns of Decay. Shakespeare's Early Histories,* p. 83.

past, a warrior nostalgia that laments the passing of war, and expresses a witty and scathing contempt for the boredom and triviality of peace".[8] It is Richard's closeness to dissembling, secrecy, treachery and the determination with which he commits his crimes, which makes vice-purists consider Richard to be an archetype of the stock character vice.[9] These critics offer a further argument for the vice-interpretation: it is the many asides and soliloquies that Richard uses to inform the audience about his true feelings and stratagems, which in a perverted way turn the audience into Richard's accomplice. It is not hard to find support for the assertion that Richard is the epitome of the vice-figure. Even the new historicist Stephen Greenblatt argues that there is ample evidence that Shakespeare exploited the cultural framework of the vice, when he shaped the character Richard:

> Shakespeare constructs Richard out of many elements in the Vice tradition: a jaunty use of asides, a delight in sharing his schemes with the audience, a grotesque appearance, a penchant for disguise, a manic energy and humor and a wickedly engaging ability to defer though not finally to escape well-deserved punishment.[10]

Contrary to the vice-purists, who look at the character Richard only from the perspective of one play, *Richard III*, others see Richard as a Machiavel, who starts to set up his stratagems already in *Henry VI*. Moving from the plays *Henry VI* to *Richard III*, the character Richard is granted an extensive time to develop. It is within this development that Richard becomes an autonomous subject and follows his own rules as Klaus Reichert argues.[11] However, all is not well since Richard's "own rules" are not accepted by society:

> The Self is the nightmare of a society, in which the old order has lost its meaning and the new order has not yet established itself properly. [...] Only a radical reduction and reconstruction of this Self as a conscientious act in the fashion of the *Ego cogitans* can introduce the autonomy of the Self in the later early modern time.[12]

Reichert sees Richard not as a Machiavellian character, but as an individual in society, deprived of love and acceptance. Richard does not

---

[8] Holderness, *Shakespeare: The Histories*, p. 81.

[9] Roe, *Shakespeare and Machiavelli*, pp. 17-18.

[10] Greenblatt, ed., *Richard III*, p. 510.

[11] See Reichert, p. 300.

[12] Reichert, p. 308 (Translation by me).

embrace evil forces in order to strive for power. His evil derives from his
exclusion from community—his quest for power is revenge on those who
exclude him:

> And am I then a man to be belov'd?
> O monstrous fault, to harbour such a thought!
> Then since this earth affords no joy to me
> But to command, to check, to o'erbear such
> As are of better person than myself,
> I'll make my heaven to dream upon the crown,
> And, whiles I live, t' account this world but hell,
> Until my misshap'd trunk that bears this head
> Be round impaled with a glorious crown (*3 Henry VI*, III.iii.163-171).

Having understood that he has "no joy" other than striving for higher
goals—the crown—Richard creates devious plots against the royal family,
propelling the dramatic action. In act five, *3 Henry VI*, Richard's solitude
is the key to his evil character:

> Then, since the heavens have shap'd my body so,
> Let hell make crook'd my mind to answer it.
> I have no brother, I am like no brother;
> And this word 'love', which greybeards call divine,
> Be resident in men like one another,
> And not in me: I am myself alone (*3 Henry VI*, V.vi.78-83).

Even as king, Richard is never fully integrated in society—he is alone and
unloved, and will remain so until the bitter end: Blunt, one of Richmond's
officers, observes that Richard's friends are false to Richard since "He
hath no friends but what are friends for fear, which in his dearest need will
fly from him" (*Richard III*, V.ii.20/1). Richard clearly lacks Machiavelli's
"remedy in times of adversity": his people's support. [13]

I believe that Richard is neither fully a vice figure nor fully a
Machiavel, he is simply beyond "humanity". Richard's quest for power
requires him on the one hand to deal with human beings but on the other
hand to ignore all humanity. If one reads the play *Richard III* in the
context of the *Henry VI* plays, Richard has a motivation—his obsession to
rule as laid out in *Henry VI*—and it becomes evident that Shakespeare
strays from the medieval tradition of the vice in the portrayal of Richard
III. Reichert thus makes a good point when he sees Richard's motivation
as derived from the circumstances not from his character—Richard is not

---

[13] See Machiavelli, p. 60.

in a battle between evil and divine forces but, he undergoes a psychological development; Shakespeare offers a milieu study of Richard.[14] Another insight into Richard is offered in *3 Henry VI*, which contradicts the vice. Here Richard is given an obvious motive for his conduct: the feeling of exclusion drives him into action: "Torment myself to catch the English crown" (III.ii.179) and so "set the murtherous Machevil to school" (*3 Henry VI*, III.ii.193). Subverting the system not only on a legal level, but also on a moral level, Richard's determination culminates in to "prove a villain" (*Richard III*, I.i.30) Though Machiavelli requests a ruler to be consciously aware of the binary good-bad opposition—an awareness Richard proves to have, although he never feels genuine remorse—Richard's commitment to do evil has little in common with Machiavelli's virtù. The character Richard is a distortion of Machiavelli's doctrine, which presents the Machiavel as someone who is committed to evil out of mere selfishness. The image of excessive murder and treachery, coupled with selfish ambition, stems little from the perception of the original but much from the distortion. Richard commits his crimes not for the sake of the welfare of his people, but only for his own sake, which again removes him from the original doctrine, since Machiavelli claims prosperity of the commonwealth to be a principal aim of a prince.[15] This assessment concurs with Emile Gasquet who concludes that the Machiavellian tyrant on stage is driven by egoistic motives rather than public interests. The main drive for a Machiavellian tyrant is selfishness; each tyrant, as Gasquet asserts, is a "monstre d'egoisme".[16] Iser agrees with this interpretation; it is the equating of Richard with the Devil that makes him:

> [a] Machiavellian force working against the legitimate order. […] While those in power see his devilry as confirmation of their legitimacy, he is happy to prey on their lack of vision. Politics becomes a game of deception, and the losers are those who believe in their own delusions.[17]

Richard himself tells us that he is obsessed with his quest for power. To satiate his power-hunger, he lets himself be driven by cruelty, symbolically presented in his desire to "hew my way out with a bloody

---

[14] See Reichert, *Der fremde Shakespeare*, p. 299 (Translation by me): *[Shakespeare] does not portray the evil as a bewitching of powers of evil […] but rather develops it from Richard's relation towards his environment.*

[15] See Machiavelli, *The Prince*, particularly the last chapter, pp. 84-88.

[16] Gasquet, *Le Courant Machiavelien,* p. 306.

[17] Iser, p. 50.

axe" (*3 Henry VI*, III.ii.181). That he does use a "bloody axe" in *Richard III* is indisputable; a fact, which results in, apart from a brief rule, rejection, fear, and disgust.

The semantics, associated with the characteristics of the vice, are reminiscent of the terminology used by Renaissance writers to describe the Machiavellian anti-hero. Richard's semantics in I.i—"villain, plots, hate, subtle, false, treacherous, secret mischief, seem, play the devil"—can be found throughout English Renaissance literature as signifiers for Machiavellianism, usually in villains, such as Barabas in the *Jew of Malta* and Bosola in the *Duchess of Malfi*. Arguably, these terms can be found in a variety of source material and stock characters, such as the vice or the classical tyrant. Yet a study which I conducted on the semantic field of Machiavelli and Machiavellianism in English Renaissance drama, has shown that terms like these can be found in conjunction with the traditional stage Machiavel throughout English Renaissance drama. The semantic field and the evidence that Shakespeare in *3 Henry VI* in fact puts *Machiavel's* name into Richard's mouth, supports the conclusion that Richard III is the epitome of the English stage Machiavel, not the Machiavellian prince.

The peak of Richard's cruelty is the murder of the two princes. This step not only deprives Richard of his closest ally, Buckingham, but also drives Richard into the isolation he was in before his ascension of the throne. Even Tyrell, helper to Richard's murders, sees the killing of the children as a "tyrannous and bloody act" (IV.iii.1), a "piteous massacre" (IV.iii.2) and "ruthless butchery" (IV.iii.5). Atrocities Tyrell himself could not commit. Even Richmond, interestingly an outsider himself and only aware of Richard's conduct from reports of others, also depicts Richard as "The wretched, bloody, and usurping boar" (V.ii.7) who commits "guilty homicide" (V.ii.18). Richard's ongoing violence clearly lacks agreement with Machiavelli's original doctrine in which he warns the prince not to let cruelty grow "in intensity".[18] Although Richard follows Machiavelli's advice and deceives, pretends to be religious and does not accept his fate but fights Fortuna, it cannot be said that Richard is the "ideal prince".[19] So I have to disagree with Robert B. Parker who claims that it is exactly this cruelty that renders Richard a Machiavellian:

---

[18] Machiavelli, p. 30.
[19] See Machiavelli, p. 57; p. 82.

Richard is a Machiavellian in the expediency aimed at personal success, not at the acquisition and maintenance of a stable state. [...] In this play we have the figure of Machiavelli without the spirit.[20]

Richard's excessive cruelty and his inability to adapt it to the circumstances are signs of the distortion. He is in no way the ideal, Machiavelli had in mind.

As a conclusion, one can say that Shakespeare has given the character Richard III ample time to develop and carefully plan his stratagems. He is not the one-sided vice figure who, without any motivation, challenges all good in the world, but he is a multi-dimensional character who tries to find happiness in life. His happiness exists however solely in the acquisition of power. The usurpation is a consequence of Richard's determined mind, a mind that Machiavelli sees in all great heroes. Yet Richard's brutality and apparent joy in this brutality, makes him stray from the path of Machiavelli's original doctrine and turn into a Machiavel. Richard's failure to cover his tracks betrays him to the other characters as the Machiavel. Since the Machiavel embodies all the fears Elizabethans had about a tyrannical sovereign, the logical consequence in the play must be that the Machiavel is ousted from society.

Works Cited

Berry, Edward I. *Patterns of Decay. Shakespeare's Early Histories.* Charlottesville: University Press of Virginia, 1975.

Campbell, Lily B. *Shakespeare's Histories. Mirrors of Elizabethan Policy.* San Marino: The Ward Richie Press, 1947.

Gasquet, Emile. *Le Courant Machiavelien. Dans la Penseé et la Littérature Anglaises du XVIe siècle.* Montréal: Didier, 1974.

Greenblatt, Stephen. "Richard III". *The Norton Shakespeare.* London: Norton and Company, 1997.

Holderness, Graham. *Shakespeare: The Histories.* Houndsmills: Macmillan Press, 2000.

Iser, Wolfgang. *Staging Politics. The Lasting Impact on Shakespeare's Histories.* New York: Columbia University Press, 1993.

Machiavelli, Niccolo. *The Prince.* Oxford: Oxford University Press, 1984.

Parker, Robert B. "The Prince and the King : Shakespeare's Machiavellian Cycle". *Revue des langues vivantes* Vol. 38 (1972), 241-53.

---

[20] Parker. "The Prince and the King: Shakespeare's Machiavellian Cycle", p. 242.

Rackin, Phyllis. *Stages of History. Shakespeare's English Chronicles.* London: Routledge, 1990.

Reichert, Klaus. *Der fremde Shakespeare.* München: Carl Hanser Verlag, 1998.

Roe, John. *Shakespeare and Machiavelli.* Cambridge: D S Brewer, 2002.

Schieder, T. "Shakespeare and Machiavelli." *Archiv für Kulturgeschichte* 34 Vols. (1951/2), pp. 131-173.

Tillyard, E. M. W. *Shakespeare's History Plays.* 2nd edn. London: Oxford UP, 1948.

—. *The Elizabethan World Picture.* 10th edn. London: Chatto & Windus, 1967.

PART TWO:

PERFORMANCE AND NEW COMPARISONS

CHAPTER SEVEN

WOMEN IN THE SHAKESPEAREAN AUDIENCE – RECOGNITION AND AUTHORITY

BRIAN SCHNEIDER

The prologue to John Fletcher's *The Woman Hater* written *c.* 1606 and first printed in 1607 begins with the word "Gentlemen"; the prologue declaimed at the revival of the play in 1638 and printed in 1649 begins "Ladies". This total change of address from the male to the female in the intervening thirty or so years reveals tellingly the increasing presence, relevance and influence of the female spectator, an influence so powerful that the new prologue jokingly wishes the women in the audience would leave; if they stay "we are undone". Women spectators expect praise from the playwright and actors, but the play itself will "Bely your Virtues, and your beauty staine".[1] It is unlikely that the Prologist is simply being ironic; the speech goes on to mention a number of Fletcher's sympathetic heroines in an attempt to mollify the women in the audience, so that in the end: "you'll find a way/How to make good the Libell in our Play". Joke or not, the text of the prologue engages the question of woman as spectator, character and judge. Looking at the audience, the Prologist observes: "you stirre not yet". If the women insist on staying, then the prologue excuses the play by explaining that it is an example of the kind of comedy "which that age/Wherein he liv'd produc'd". In other words the kind of drama produced in 1606 was disparaging to women in a way that would not happen in 1638. All this of course is good rollicking fun, but there is an underlying acknowledgment that women spectators can be addressed and made complicit with the actors and playwright in the extra-dramatic ideas explored in the framing material of prologues and epilogues.

Whether there is an analogous cultural shift towards a deepening of women's authority outside of the theatrical experience is not within the

---

[1] Quoted from John Fletcher, *The Woman Hater*, prologue, line 1, 1607 and 1649 editions respectively.

scope of this discussion, though there is a body of thought that suggests the contrary. Sara Heller Mendelson and Patricia Crawford, for example, query: "Why [...] did certain women manage to assert formal civil and political rights at the beginning of our period, and why did these rights deteriorate or disappear over the course of the seventeenth century"?[2] Whilst this deterioration may be true in the general community, it is the contention of this essay that, at least in the theatre, women were recognised as an important constituent of any audience and were often addressed in prologues and epilogues to solicit their approval and their influence in furthering a particular play's continued success.

The title page of the 1640 edition of *Love's Mistress* by Thomas Heywood (1634) boasts that it has been "three times presented before their two excellent Majesties, within the space of eight dayes" and publicly acted by the "Queen's Comedians" at The Phoenix. The play's first prologue for the stage presentation begins with Cupid discussing the elaborate treatment afforded to "State Ladies" (and "Great Men") in Roman times. Such treatment, the speaker regrets, is not available from the present group of players: "Although we cannot meet you with like"; instead, it is the bare play that is offered, which Cupid describes as "His sweete and dearest Mistris" and which he continues to refer to as "she". The whole prologue as well as the presentation to follow is thus feminised – there is no specific allusion to the male section of the audience except by the implication of the words "Great men" spoken earlier.

A further prologue, also delivered by Cupid, was written for a performance of the play at Denmark House in The Strand to celebrate the King's birthday. After lavishing twelve lines of praise on His Majesty, exactly the same number of lines is expended on fulsome compliments to the Goddess of Love and, by implication, the Queen, followed by an almost absent-minded last line in which we are reminded that it is the "Great King" in whose honour the performance is actually given. The equality of praise is at once recognition of the importance of the feminine, and an astute diplomatic manoeuvre by Heywood to acknowledge the Queen, a move which would certainly please her husband Charles I. In a third Prologue (again addressed to their Majesties) Cupid gives pride of place to the Queen, calling her "A Presence that from Venus takes all power".[3] Later the prologue brings both King and Queen together as an earthly Jove and Juno, allowing them an equality which once more suggests gracious diplomacy and a recognition of at least one woman's

---

[2] Mendelson and Crawford, *Women in Early Modern England, 1550-1720*, p. 4.
[3] Heywood, *Love's Mistress or The Queen's Masque*, prologue 5.

authority, further emphasised in the epilogue when the goddess herself is
invoked: "Juno the Marriage queene, shall bless your bed". The earthly
Juno of the prologue thus gives way to this more heavenly figure and the
symbolic power given to the female is emphasised. Whilst the lines in
recognition of the feminine are addressed here solely to the Queen and
cannot be seen as a *general* acknowledgment of female authority, the
manner in which the feminine is invoked may be seen as part of the
cumulative effect of the mention of women in prologues and epilogues at
work in the period and of the increasingly urgent perception of the role of
women as audience members. By the way this private performance "In the
presence of sundry Foreign Ambassadors" according to the title page, was
possibly given under the alternative title of *The Queen's Masque*, a further
acknowledgement of the pervading presence of the female.

Two totally opposing positions regarding women's status in the drama
of the early seventeenth century point to the difficulty of achieving
anything resembling a consensus of women's real power or otherwise in
the period. For Linda Woodbridge the first decade "had witnessed
unprecedented misogyny in the drama".[4] She is explicit in her view of this
misogyny: "the early Jacobean theatre produced a body of plays which
delineated with a savage cynicism the lewdness, infidelity, aggression,
shallowness, cupidity and deceit of a legion of faithless citizens' wives,
insatiable widows, and homicidal whores".[5] For Juliet Dusinberre "The
drama from 1590 to 1625 is feminist in sympathy".[6] She goes further:
"The dramatists' adoption of radical attitudes to women's rights is
consistent not only with their need to please the audience of whom a
sizeable part was female [...] but also consistent with their [...] own need
to repudiate conservative judgments on their calling".[7] This is a view to
which the argument of this presentation is more sympathetic. Constance
Jordan tries to steer a middle course, claiming that whilst some women
had power, most did not and that there was a "failure of sixteenth-century
feminist debate to produce any social change".[8] Jean Hagen and Pearl
Hogrefe both detect a decline in the status of women after Elizabeth's

---

[4] Woodbridge, *Women and the English Renaissance: Literature and the Nature of
Womankind, 1540-1620*, p. 249.
[5] Ibid, p. 249.
[6] Dusinberre, *Shakespeare and the nature of women*, p. 5.
[7] Ibid, p. 5.
[8] Jordan, *Renaissance Feminism: literary texts and political models, pp.* 301-2.
She invokes the *Hic Mulier* and *Haec Vir* debates to support her conclusion.

death.[9] Dympna Callaghan also finds difficulty in deciding whether or not women could demonstrate any real autonomy. Though she insists that: "...*presence cannot be equated with representation any more than representation can be equated with inclusion*", she also observes "recognition of women's oppression does not *de facto* render women abject victims of patriarchal culture or deny them agency".[10] Of the position of the female in the period, Virginia Woolf claims: "Imaginatively she is of the highest importance; practically she is completely insignificant".[11] Safely ensconced in the pages of a book, adored in the lines of a poem or romance, acted by a boy, women in the theatre and elsewhere appear to be successfully contained by a dominant patriarchy. But we are once more faced with the paradox that the sites of women's apparent marginalisation, or even exclusion, are also the sites of possible subversion and assertion of influence. If boys did play women's parts, they apparently did it so well that the sight of female actresses on the Continent produced Coryat's famous remark that "they performed it with as good a grace, action, gesture and whatsoever convenient for a player, as ever I saw any masculine actor".[12] What Coryat is suggesting is that boys could play women, or at least his notion of women, perfectly. If boys could act this well, perhaps they could also occasionally represent a true female voice. In addition, "female" characters who occasionally proclaim the prologue or epilogue or who interrupt these framing devices, even though played by boys, also put forward arguments on behalf of women which directly inform the spectators of, and thus involve them in, the ongoing debate about women's place in society. Female dramatists, such as Margaret Cavendish, make even stronger assaults on the prevailing ideologies and on the construction of women in the period, though in

---

[9] Gagen, *The New Woman: Her Emergence in English Drama 1600-1730*, p. 16. Also see Hogrefe, *Tudor Woman: Commoners and Queens*, p. 142, which asserts: "King James gave no encouragement to the literary pursuits of women like Elizabeth Carey, Mary Sidney Herbert and Lucy Russell. His court [...] had no intellectual life for women".

[10] Callaghan, *Shakespeare Without Women: Representing Gender and Race on the Renaissance Stage*, p. 9.

[11] Woolf, *A Room of One's Own*, p. 43.

[12] Coryat, *Coryat's Crudities*, p. 247. Coryat also mentions in the same breath that women had been known to act in London. However, even after the Restoration and the introduction of female actors, there was resistance and a perception that women could not act female part as well as men. Snarl, in Thomas Shadwell's *The Virtuoso* (1676), a character who wallows in nostalgia, comments: "I can never endure to see Plays, since Women came on the stage. Boys are better by half", I. ii. 153-4.

Cavendish's case there is uncertainty about the amount of freedom she claims or even desires. Though women playwrights during the period circulated plays through manuscript, publication or closet performance only, and did not enjoy presentation in the professional theatre, nevertheless the dissemination of texts they did achieve gave them a voice of sorts, even if only in a minor key. Other forms of women's writing - poems, letters, translations, and diaries - widen the promulgation of women's claim to some autonomy, even if such autonomy was often mediated by recognition of, and adherence to, a patriarchal view. The argument here suggests that the inclusion, in prologues and epilogues, of women as members of the audience and the significant occasions in which women are specifically addressed in these texts, afford a *public* recognition of their ability to contribute to the theatrical experience.

Andrew Gurr, describing the period following the opening of the first professional theatres, has suggested that "women from every section of society went to plays", and that "a plentiful supply of women playgoers is there throughout the period".[13] Their importance as spectators, according to Richard Levin, depended "on whether they were regarded by the playwrights and acting companies as a constituency whose interests and feelings should be considered".[14] Though often stereotyped, women were occasionally more selectively anatomised, as in the first prologue to Ben Jonson's *Epicoene*, in which women were differentiated as "ladies", "waiting wench", "citie-wives" and "daughters of white-Friars".[15] A vital part of the evidence regarding the presence and status of women as spectators, as Levin recognises, resides in the prologues and epilogues of the period, a number of which he quotes. His conclusion is somewhat sweeping: "Except for the special situation in the Caroline private theatres, men seem to have dominated the audiences and the playwrights' conceptions of those audiences".[16] Even if this is accepted, the "special situation" to which he alludes is interesting, in that it points to the growing awareness of women as an important component of the audience, even if only in a particular section of the professional theatre, a section however in which a fair number of the playwrights of the time were represented. It was in the private theatres that men like Davenant and Killigrew made their marks and, at the Restoration, Davenant in particular was given a major role in the revival of the theatrical tradition, in which women were

---

[13] Gurr, *Playgoing in Shakespeare's London*, p. 58.
[14] Levin, "Women in the Renaissance Theatre", p. 169.
[15] Jonson, *Epicoene*, prologue 21-24.
[16] Richard Levin, "Women in the Renaissance Theatre", p. 174.

to prove even more influential, this time as writers and actors, as well as spectators.

Callaghan is less sanguine about the treatment of women in the new professional theatre as opposed to their presence in earlier dramatic presentations. She insists that the Renaissance theatre "became a specific and more absolute site of exclusion than in the cyclical, ritual cycles of the medieval era, records of which document payments to women who may have been engaged in actual performance".[17] In her determination to demonstrate that there was no female participation in the theatre that was not mediated by men, she ignores those moments when, in prologues, epilogues and inductions, women are specifically called upon to judge the theatrical experience presented. She also ignores the occasions when women characters that deliver the prologues and epilogues demand and appear to receive power. Instead she attempts to turn the notion of female authority on its head: speaking of women's excessively emotional response to plays, described by men such as Thomas Heywood and Anthony Munday, she asserts of such response that the "violent female reaction" which "was the measure of performance in a theatre founded on the symbolic violence of excluding women from the stage, neither invariably places women in a position of power nor guarantees women's pleasure".[18] At one point, however, even she appears to recognise the possibility of a pro-women argument, noting that "while the premise of all-male performance is misogynist [...] in its execution the performance of femininity might even champion women".[19] And, as far as pleasure is concerned, men also cannot be guaranteed this and Callaghan's words do not preclude the possibility of occasional success in the claiming of authority, or at least of influence by the female. Nor does Callaghan take into account those prologues and epilogues which carefully differentiate the audience by gender and try to accommodate both. Rosalind, in *As You Like It*, significantly states in her new role as the Epilogist: "I'll begin with the women" after which she brings in the male members of the audience before proceeding to dissolve gender in a welter of paradoxical suggestion: "If I were a woman" he/she declares.[20] In the epilogue to the second part of *Henry IV*, the playwright hopes "All the gentlewomen here have forgiven me; if the gentlemen will not, then the gentlemen do not agree with the gentlewomen, which was never seen in such an assembly"

---

[17] Callaghan, *Shakespeare Without Women*, p. 15.
[18] Ibid, p. 162.
[19] Ibid, p. 162.
[20] This echoes the play's persistent word-play surrounding "if" (cf. Touchstone: "Your If is the only peacemaker; much virtue in If").

(20-23), whilst in *Henry VIII*, the last framing speech looks for the "merciful construction of good women" (10). In these last two cases the appeal to women suggests at the same time that they will be more sympathetic than the men to the playwright's endeavours and, perhaps stereotypically, that they are more easily pleased. Certainly, the prologue to Fletcher's *Love's Pilgrimage* adopts the latter view: "Ten to one/We please the women". At the same time Fletcher jokingly emphasises female influence: "and I'd know that man/Follows not their example"[21]. Lodowick Carlell's epilogue to *Arviragus and Philicia* (1636) asserts more strongly that "The gentler sex [...] can make a Poem live or Poet dye".[22]

John Fletcher's prologue to the play *Rule a Wife and Have a Wife* licensed in 1624 and played at the Blackfriars, addresses the female spectator almost exclusively and whilst it is often condescending: "Ladies be not angry if you see/A fresh young beauty, wanton and too free,/Seeke to abuse her Husband" it nevertheless suggests an anxiety about women's acceptance of this kind of play and looks to soliciting their tolerance for the playwright's endeavours.[23] Ben Jonson's 1624 play *The Staple of News*, begins with an induction in which The Prologist is interrupted by four Gossips who claim that they have only come to the theatre "to see and be seen".[24] Although Jonson satirises these four ladies he also uses one of them as a kind of Chorus during the play, putting forward Jonson's own views of the audience and the players. In the epilogue to Lodowick Carlell's *The Passionate Lovers* (1638) the ladies of the audience are addressed first: "As those who judge of Lovers actions best".[25] Whilst this may appear once again to suggest that women respond stereotypically to a play, the epilogue goes on to confirm that the female spectator's favourable reaction to the main actor in the play means that "Our Author hath his chiefest end obtain'd". James Shirley, in the prologue to his play *The Imposture* (1640), addresses the men in the audience as "Our judges, Great Commissioners of wit" but he ends the text with an address to the Ladies of whom he says "In all his Poems, you have been his care" and observes: "the wise/Will learn to like by looking on your eyes".[26] Whilst once more stereotypically suggesting that women are more emotional than men and actually saying that they are prone to blushing, Shirley

---

[21] Fletcher, *Love's Pilgrmage*, prologue, 11-12.

[22] Carlell, *Arviragus and Philicia*, epilogue.

[23] Fletcher, *Rule a Wife and Have a Wife*, prologue, 9-11.

[24] Jonson, *The Staple of News*, induction, 9-10.

[25] Carlell, *The Passionate Lovers*, epilogue, 2.

[26] Shirley, *The Imposture*, prologue, 22, 28-9.

nevertheless asserts that women's less cold and objective response to a dramatist's work is perhaps the more productive.

Most of the plays mentioned so far were staged at the Globe or the Blackfriars (sometimes at both venues) and do not represent all the prologues and epilogues which mention women or which invoke the feminine via the Muses or the Queen, or classical figures. These two theatres were perhaps less engaged in promoting the idea of the importance of women spectators as judges of the plays presented, than in simply registering their presence and their hoped for reaction to the dramatic experience. But that they did register and applaud that presence is clear.

In however limited a form, therefore, what becomes increasingly apparent in the prologues and epilogues of the period is that women gradually increased their influence as spectators and such influence was acknowledged by the playwrights in their appeals to the female members of the audience to accept their offerings, occasionally allowing women to be the judges of their plays and increasingly introducing the feminine at the outset of the theatrical experience, an experience heralded by the prologue and later summed up by the epilogue. In addition, some playwrights occasionally, but significantly, used female characters to deliver such texts. The tendency to include the feminine grows in urgency during the period and the prologues and epilogues that embrace the idea of feminine presence and importance increase in number and insistence.

Scholars, examining the role of women in this period, point to the ways in which some women either subvert patriarchy or find themselves a space within the prevailing culture, which gives them (apparent) authority, a (limited) power, or at least an influential voice. I have argued that in a significant number of prologues and epilogues of the early English theatre, women are actually being offered such a voice, in a *popular public place*. The offer may at times be grudging or ironic; it may be accompanied by stereotyping; it is certainly a fleeting moment, lasting for the duration of the performance only. But, as has been suggested, the offer of some autonomy becomes stronger and is stated more often as the period progresses. In the anxious debates about women's roles in society, the playwrights add their contribution via these extra-dramatic texts as well as in the actual plays themselves. The relatively smooth transition from woman as spectator only, to woman as actress *and* spectator soon after the Restoration may, in part at least, be linked to the growing recognition that women were an increasingly important part of the entire theatrical experience in the Renaissance period.

Works Cited

All early-modern texts referenced have been accessed on "Early English Books Online", at http://eebo.chadwyck.com/home.

Aughterson, Kate. *Renaissance Woman: Constructions of Femininity in England.* London: Routledge, 1995.

Brown, Pamela Allen and Parolin, Peter eds. *Women Players in England 1500 – 1660: Beyond the All-Male Stage.* Aldershot: Ashgate, 2005.

Callaghan, Dympna. *Shakespeare Without Women: Representing Gender and Race on the Renaissance Stage.* London: Routledge, 2000.

—. *Women and Gender in Renaissance Tragedy.* Atlantic Highlands: Humanities Press International, 1989.

Coryat, Thomas. *Coryat's Crudities.* 1611.

Dusinberre, Juliet. *Shakespeare and the Nature of Women.* London: Macmillan, 1996.

Ferguson, Margaret W., Quilligan, Maureen, and Vickers, Nancy J eds., *Rewriting the Renaissance: The Discourse of Sexual Difference in Early Modern Europe.* Chicago: University of Chicago Press, 1986.

Findlay, Alison. *A Feminist Perspective on Renaissance Drama.* Oxford: Blackwell, 1999.

Gagen, Jean. *The New Woman: Her Emergence in English Drama 1600-1730.* New York: Twayne, 1954.

Gurr, Andrew. *Playgoing in Shakespeare's London.* Cambridge: Cambridge University Press, 1987.

Hogrefe, Pearl. *Tudor Woman: Commoner and Queens.* Ames: Iowa, 1975.

Jankowski, Theadora A. *Women in Power in the Early Modern Drama.* Urbana: University of Illinois Press, 1992.

Jordan, Constance. *Renaissance Feminism: literary texts and political models.* Ithaca: Cornell University Press, 1990

Levin, Richard. "Women in the Renaissance Theatre Audience." *Shakespeare Quarterly* 40, (1989): pp. 165-74.

McLean, Ian. *The Renaissance Notion of Woman: A Study in the Fortunes of Scholasticism and Medical Science in European Intellectual Life.* Cambridge: Cambridge University Press, 1980.

McManus, Clare. *Women on the Renaissance Stage: Anne of Denmark and Female Masquerading in the Stuart Court (1590-1619).* Manchester: Manchester University Press, 2002.

Mendelson, Sara Heller and Patricia Crawford. *Women in Early Modern England, 1550 – 1720.* Oxford: Clarendon Press, 1998.

Shadwell, Thomas. *The Virtuoso*, ed. by Marjorie Hope Nicholson and David Stuart Rhodes. London: Edward Arnold, 1966.

Traub, Valerie, Lindsay M. Caplan and Dympna Callaghan, eds. *Feminist Readings of Early Modern Culture*. Cambridge: Cambridge University Press, 1996.

Woodbridge, Linda. *Women and the English Renaissance: Literature and the Nature of Womankind, 1540 – 1620*. Brighton: Harvester, 1984.

Woolf, Virginia. *A Room of One's Own*. London: Hogarth Press, 1929.

CHAPTER EIGHT

DIS-PLAYING HISTORY:
THE CASE OF SHAKESPEARE'S GLOBE

KELLY JONES

Linger your patience on, and we'll digest
Th'abuse of distance, *force* – perforce - a play.
—*Henry V*, II.Chorus.31-2, my italics.

The Chorus in Shakespeare's *Henry V* provides one of the most famous examples of an appeal to an audience to play with the players and assist in the creation of an imaginary play-world. On the surface the Chorus provides an insistently apologetic allusion to the inadequacies of the spectacle of representation – the inability of a few men to represent a thousand, the incompetence of the Globe theatre to contain the fields of Agincourt, and repeatedly calls upon the audience's complicity and their "imaginary puissance" to sustain the lie (I.Prologue.25). The creation of the play relies upon the collaborative effort between players and play-goers in an act of theatrical play that apparently relies heavily upon the audience's imaginations and their ability "to piece out our imperfections with [their] thoughts" (I.Prologue.23). However, whilst it is reliant upon the audience's imaginary forces, the Chorus also engineers a regulatory control over their creative capacities, and the authority of the Chorus's honeyed words acquires power through the audience's complicit subjectivity, and he/she directs their imaginary puissance to "*force* - perforce - a play" upon them. The rules of the play between audience and players are not subject to a fair and equal negotiation and if the audience are to participate in the creation of the play, their participation is premised upon the players' rules alone. The audience can either choose to comply or refuse to participate in the game of make-believe in which the rules of play are already outlined by the Chorus as he/she permits them to share in the theatrical mediation of history – a history that is controlled, as the

Prologue to Shakespeare's *Troilus and Cressida* announces, by "author's pen and actor's voice" (Prologue.24).[1]

The audience can either play along with the Chorus as he/she plays upon their imaginary thoughts, or they can decline to play the game, resist his control and approach the glorified show of Henry's "victory" with a more critical suspicion. The audience is not completely unarmed and if there is an instrument that allows the audience to foster a critical and discerning distance from the glorification of history, it comes in the form of the Chorus, the master of manipulation himself. The Chorus's meta-theatricality exposes his own dubious authority that is evidently premised upon the manipulative power of the process of storytelling itself, and the harnessing of theatrical play, as he stage-manages the representation of his-(s)tory.

Shakespeare's use of meta-theatrical devices can be seen to invoke a critical perspicacity on the part of an audience, arousing their awareness of how they are being forced into an act of play and how much they are bound by certain rules. Rules confer a level of control, and control appears to be an important condition of the appropriation of play. Moreover, it is significant how the limitations of control are imposed upon play: whether all the participants in the act of playing participate in the construction of the rules of the play, or whether the rules of the play are imposed upon them to display an agency of power through appropriated theatrical play.

This idea of "display" requires some attention here. The word "display" hails from the Old French/Latinate "despleier" ("to unfold") and, according to *The New Oxford Dictionary of English*, it means, in its verbal form, to "make a prominent exhibition of (something) in a place where it can be easily seen", and, as a noun, it signifies "a performance, show, or event intended for public entertainment".[2] To somewhat crudely and synthetically deconstruct the word to allow "dis" to operate as a prefix for the word "play" is highly pertinent:

> dis- prefix 1. expressing negation [...] 2. denoting reversal or absence of an action or state [...] 3. denoting removal of something [...] 4. expressing completeness or intensification of an unpleasant or unattractive action.[3]

As artificial as such a deconstruction may appear, the meanings inherent within the term, "dis-play" can be exploited to provide what appears to be

---

[1] Weimann has examined the connotations of this remark in his study, *Author's Pen and Actor's Voice*.

[2] Pearsall, ed., *The New Oxford Dictionary of English*, p. 532.

[3] Pearsall, ed., *The New Oxford Dictionary of English*, p. 523.

a very apt description of the word "display". "Display" ("dis-play") signifies a "negation", "lack" or "deprivation" or even a "removal" of the more unrestricted anarchic energies of "play" and the faculties of participatory creativity and its expression. Somewhat paradoxically, the prefix does not always have to express a negation, and can also indicate "completeness or intensification of the action", and to this end, may be interpreted to signify an intensification of play in its more concentrated or directed form. The "play" inherent in "display" is tightly controlled as "play" that superficially appears to incorporate elements of interaction and to encourage a shared participation in the play-construction, whilst it in fact negates any truly communal and democratic activity. Such play is designed to direct and control the involvement of at least some of its participants implicated in the act of play, whether they are spectators or performers.

Dis-play boasts a powerful hegemonic agency over the projection and mediation of an image. Michel Foucault draws upon the connection between power and display in *Discipline and Punish: The Birth of the Prison*; in reference to his discussion of the capital punishment system as an spectacle of hegemonic power enacted and enforced upon the transgressing subject's corporeal body as a display of power, he states: "Traditionally, power was what was seen, what was shown and what was manifested and paradoxically, found the principle of its force in the movements by which it deployed that force".[4] To contextualise this assertion, in the masques and pageants of the Elizabethan and Stuart courts, the currency of visual spectacle was implemented to create an exhibition of the Sovereign's power through a display of aesthetic presentation that was subjected to a rigid authoritative control over the image to be viewed by the audience. To this extent, "display" contains a visual and material element that can be controlled more tightly than the imaginative connotations of "play".

As this essay seeks to demonstrate, questions concerning the relationship between play and the rules imposed upon it are highly resonant in application to the more contemporary theatrical experience offered at Shakespeare's Globe in London. I wish to explore and at least stimulate questions as to the ideological connotations that lie behind the relationship between theatrical play and cultural, historical and hegemonic display at the playhouse. Although seen at the outset as a theatre that will unfetter the audience from the constraints of behaviour imposed in the darkened theatre auditoriums of the proscenium-arch theatres, and that will

---

[4] Foucault, *Discipline and Punish: The Birth of the Prison*, p. 187.

liberate the play-texts of Shakespeare and his contemporaries, enabling audiences, scholars and practitioners to more coherently understand "how Shakespeare's plays worked in their original performance conditions", as this essay argues, the idea of such "liberation" is tangled up in fraudulent ideals, and that the audience at the Globe, herded like sheep, simply exchanges one set of rules, one kind of display, for another.

Inspired by Sam Wanamaker's vision to reconstruct a conjectural replica of the original playhouse where Shakespeare's company performed four hundred years ago, the New Globe opened in 1995, and since then has continued to draw in theatre-goers, theatre aficionados and tourists alike. A place now exists to endorse the permissible experimentation of placing Shakespeare's plays under the speculative conditions of performance for which they were originally created in the sixteenth and seventeenth centuries.

The stage, cleared of the trappings of mise-en-scène and the scenic frame of the proscenium arch stage, appears to operate as a space conducive to the imaginative capabilities of the audience, who, under the simulated performance conditions of the Elizabethan-Jacobean stage are encouraged to "play" with the performers to create and sustain the fictional world of the play. Stimulated by the words of the performers, the audience is asked to believe that the stage has transformed into a sea-shore in Illyria, a castle at Elsinore or the Forest of Arden; and to, as the Chorus in *Henry V* requests, "piece out our imperfections with your thoughts" (Prologue.23).

The staging of the plays at the new Globe Theatre has begun to reveal just how great an impact the physical and material factors of the theatrical space might have had upon the nature and the style of the performance. In his essay, "Staging at the Globe", Andrew Gurr asserts:

> The Globe offers the opportunity of making a variety of new measurements, ranging from how long it takes to walk offstage, to the acoustics of a soliloquy directed at only one section of the total surround of the audience [...] Measurements such as these need to be made as we try to gain information from the experiment of reconstructing Shakespeare's theatre that will help our understanding of his plays.[5]

Undeniably the space has potential to inspire investigation into the original staging practices of Shakespeare and his contemporaries; to mediate plays such as *Hamlet, King Lear*, and *Twelfth Night*, under the speculated performance conditions of the original theatres. It has also

---

[5] Gurr, "Staging at the Globe" in *Shakespeare's Globe Rebuilt,* p. 159.

opened up an increased sensitivity and spatial-consciousness for academics and theatre practitioners alike. The new Globe Theatre has thereby created a *playground* and *display-ground* for theatre historians as an "interactive museum" where the space is revered for seemingly permitting actors and audience to enjoy the experience of, what Raphael Samuel has called "living history [which] allows us to play games with the past and to pretend that we are at home in it, ignoring the limitations of time and space by reincarnating it in the here-and-now".[6]

"Living history", as Samuel explains, can be used to "bring history to life" by allowing an audience or reader to engage with a simulated reconstruction of the past. The problem with such an "interactive museum", however, is that it tends to display the space as a historical document, setting-up an ideologically controlled and contrived celebration and canonisation of the historical and institutionalised values embedded in the space. In this respect the theatre may be *seen* as simply another building of historical interest, rather like Anne Hathaway's house in Stratford-upon-Avon - a theatre "museum" rather than a place of entertainment. Catherine Belsey identifies this problem: "'Living history' is synchronic: it isolates a specific moment of the past and erases, ostensibly at least, everything that has happened since".[7] The space itself is *displayed*, presented as a historical curiosity, inhabiting a realm of historical and spatial "otherness" from the other concrete modern buildings that sprawl across London's South-Bank, and the Globe with its round timber-frame understandably fails to blend in with its neighbouring architecture.

I am not the first to draw attention to the Globe's status as a potential museum or living monument. The theme was taken up several years ago in an article in which William B. Worthen critiqued the problems of manufacturing the Globe as a Shakespearean theme-park: he aptly calls it "Bard-World."[8] Nevertheless, despite offering an insightful critique into the ideological assumptions behind the Globe project, I believe that Worthen's argument falls victim to the very essentialism he has tried to efface when he concludes: "it's *our* Globe, necessarily part of how *we*

---

[6] Samuel, *Theatres of Memory: Vol 1: Past and Present in Contemporary Culture*, pp. 195-6.
[7] Belsey, "Reading Cultural History", *Reading the Past: Literature and History*, pp. 105-6.
[8] Worthen, "Reconstructing the Globe: Constructing Ourselves", p. 41. Worthen acknowledges that his use of the term derives from David Patrick Stearns, "Reconstructed Globe Provides Theater in the Real", *USA Today*, 13 June 1997, 11A.

imagine the great (w)hole of history".[9] His allusion to "our" and "we" assumes a collective ownership over the theatrical experience provided at the Globe with the same fraudulent rhetoric as *Henry V*'s Chorus.

If "we" are, as Worthen suggests, "to imagine the great (w)hole of history", piecing out any imperfections with "our" thoughts, then, like the audience of *Henry V*, our imagination is subject to ideological control, directed by the architectural design of the playhouse itself. The audience's imagination is certainly directed towards an "authoritative" projection of cultural and performance history, which is as ephemeral as the existence of the Forest of Arden or the fields of Agincourt.

The audience members who enter the space can "play" at being Elizabethan spectators – participants of a historical and cultural *display* – through what Peter Thomson has called "the collision of a holy space with its unholy visitors".[10] With the opportunity to radically subvert the behavioural constraints and the silent spectatorship usually expected within the darkened auditoriums of the proscenium arch theatres, the members of the audience are in danger of becoming somewhat self-indulgent in their response to the play, waiting expectantly for a cue from the actors to release laughter, a hiss or a round of applause. In belonging to the space, the persons of the audience can also potentially become a consenting component of the display. One reviewer, Alistair Macaulay described the contrived and somewhat formulaic lengths the performers will go to in order to stage a reaction from the audience for the purpose of allowing them to feel a part of the experience of being a constituent of the play:

> The Globe players have discovered how to play this audience to perfection, if not the plays they happen to be performing. The method is simple: deliver everything like Christmas pantomime. Play broadly for laughs; wait for each laugh; invite the audience to boo or hiss the baddies; have cast members rush comically through the audience. The recipe works, only too well.[11]

The audience has not necessarily been given an organic presence in the mediation of Shakespeare's plays in performance; rather it has been

---

[9] Worthen, "Reconstructing the Globe: Constructing Ourselves", 45. Worthen's reference to the "Great Hole of History" is inspired by its use in Suzan-Lori Parks's *The American Play* (1994) and he describes the expression as "a replica both of the fullness (whole) of history, and its undoing, its absence (hole) in representation", p. 34.

[10] Thomson, "The New Globe: Monument or Portent?", p. 191.

[11] Macaulay, review of *The Maid's Tragedy* and *A Chaste Maid in Cheapside*.

scripted in. The spectators are reduced to the level of performing dogs, rewarded by the experience of feeling a part of the performance and part of the cultural display of the space itself. I witnessed an example of an actor staging an audience reaction myself a few years ago: Mark Rylance, playing the role of Richard II, spoke the famous line "For God's sake, let us sit down upon the ground,/and tell sad stories of the death of kings", (III.ii.151-2) as he sat down on the stage and asserted the line pertly to the audience and seemed to wait expectantly for the tumultuous applause that would follow; anticipating the audience's reaction before the scene could proceed.

The populist left-wing pseudo-democracy behind the Globe project exploits the freedom from the despotic proscenium arch, inciting the actors to engage directly with the audience. The performers are permitted and even encouraged to resist the canonicity and textual authority of the Shakespearean play-scripts through extemporising asides to the audience. Simon Edge in a scathing review of the 2005 summer production of *Pericles* records that Patrice Naiambana, who played Gower, the narrator, saw fit to *ad lib*, declaring to the audience: "If you came here for art, you've come to the wrong place. At the Globe we do lowbrow".[12] This assertion outraged a number of theatre critics who accused the Globe of "dumbing down" and perhaps could be perceived as an insult to the audience and an assault on their intelligence as cultural consumers. Furthermore, such a bold statement, although possibly exposing an attempt to re-create the same impertinence and irreverence towards the dramatic script of a Kemp or a Tarlton, worryingly reveals a lack of compromise between an elusive concept of "high" art and low-brow tumbling tricks. There seems, somewhat perversely, no room for the mingling of kings with clowns.

On the other side of the coin, the "right-wing conservatism" of capitalising on the Shakespeare industry by introducing "Bard-world" attempts to recreate the traditional modes of performance in which Shakespeare's plays were originally produced.

Whilst displaying its visual "otherness" from the other theatre buildings of London's West End, the Globe playhouse is also subjected to a display of institutionalised and ideologically-enforced cultural values as the theatrical reconstruction of the theatre where the plays of the iconic genius, William Shakespeare, were staged four hundred years ago. The space is in danger of becoming a living monument; a fetishized object of a quasi-religious celebration of the Bard of Avon and his cohorts. The New

---

[12] Edge, *Daily Express*, June 3, 2005.

Globe theatre could display, what John Drakakis in 1995 (when the building was nearing completion) called:

> the fabrication of tradition replete with a quasi-religious iconography, and a shrine at which to worship [...] The building will become the site of a séance designed to resurrect in certain conditions the spirits of Burbage, Heminge, Condell, Will Kemp, Robert Armin, Shakespeare, of course, and now Sam Wanamaker.[13]

David Wiles responds with more optimistic idealism:

> The new Globe offers [...] the spectator a reassuring sense that he or she inhabits a structured "world" or "cosmos", and not the fragmentary condition of postmodernity. It provides a physical centre around which values can be constructed. It may indeed be the case that Shakespeare's Globe is a calculated artifice, yet the faith that Shakespeare was the genius of the second millennium has its effect on the audience. And the behaviour of the audience is a main part of the performance. The problem with Drakakis' cultural materialism is that, for all its moral and intellectual rigour, it cannot account for what makes an intense theatrical experience.[14]

There is no denying the intensity of the theatrical experience that the Globe offers, yet I must interrogate the naiveté of Wiles's assertion in its unquestioning acceptance that the playhouse offers a fallaciously reassuring structured "world" or "cosmos" in a contemporary world that apparently offers none. It assumes the universal acknowledgement of the existence of a "fragmentary condition of postmodernity", whilst also asserting a sense of nostalgia and a glorification of a "simpler" time when it is presumed the world made more sense. It is highly precarious to assume that such a stable "structure" existed unequivocally and unambiguously in the Elizabethan age. The idea that the new Globe can provide "a physical centre around which values can be constructed" (or even re-constructed) assumes the same essentialist conception of an all-encompassing and universally-accepted hegemony of an Elizabethan World Picture that has been so vehemently attacked by the schools of New Historicism and Cultural Materialism over the past several decades.[15]

---

[13] Drakakis, "Dr Strangelove or how I learnt to put my trust in the Globe and set fire to my dreams".

[14] Wiles, *A Short History of the Western Performance Space*, p. 60.

[15] Tillyard's *The Elizabethan World Picture* suggested a generalised dictum of how the "educated Elizabethan man" understood the world around him, and how all "intelligent" people subscribed, unquestioningly, to a set of values and beliefs.

If, by entering into a "structured" space, the audience can temporarily "play" at being a community within the playhouse walls, perhaps they should be encouraged, at the very least, to cultivate a discerning consciousness as to the ideological and cultural resonances that lie behind this process of play. Shakespeare himself has made feasible such critical perspicacity on the part of the audience by providing meta-theatrical devices to mediate the theatrical experience. When Shakespeare's company, in 1599, moved into their new home at the Globe, *Henry V* was one of the first plays to be staged in this new theatre. It is the Chorus of this play who commanded attention as he spoke the opening lines of the play and worked to destabilise and resist the complacency of the play-going experience, even as he called upon the complicity of the audience for its creation.

If scholars are to learn something new about how Shakespeare used his theatre to assess the ideological values implicit in its material conditions of production, maybe a study is necessary into the meta-theatrical devices such as the Chorus's function to expose the playfulness behind the display. Theatrical display will not and should not be restrained by an ideological agenda and therefore transcends such ideological agency even from within it, deconstructing and exposing all display as a pretentious appropriation of play used to sanction a specific ideological agenda. The Elizabethan and Jacobean playwrights ostensibly delighted in using meta-theatrical devices such as prologues, chorus figures, and induction sequences to interrogate the processes of play, initiating a concern with theatrical space and the ideological constituents of its frame. These explicitly playful meta-theatrical figures demonstrate how, whilst their theatrical playfulness manipulates the playgoer's experience of the theatrical event to synthetically "digest the abuse of [historical] distance" to "force a play"; they similarly display to us how Shakespeare's texts, regardless of their performance conditions, persist in challenging the audience's encounter with that same theatrical and historical experience. [16] It is this persistence that provides the verve of Shakespeare's plays in performance and perhaps this is the innovatory insight the third Globe can offer regarding the workings of Shakespeare's plays both in the original Globe and today's playhouse – a revitalised interest and fascination regarding the premise of its theatricality.

---

[16] James N. Loehlin makes a similar assertion in *Shakespeare in Performance: Henry V*, suggesting that the problematic historical display of Henry V as hero could open up "a greater emphasis on the play's concern with its own making, a self-consciously theatrical approach in which the audience would identify more with the process of representation than with what was represented", p. 168.

Works Cited

Belsey, Catherine. "Reading Cultural History" In *Reading the Past: Literature and History*. Edited by Tamsin Spargo. Basingstoke: Palgrave, 2000.

Drakakis, John. "Dr Strangelove or how I learnt to put my trust in the Globe and set fire to my dreams". *The European English Messenger* 4.1 (1995).

Edge, Simon. Review of *Pericles* at Shakespeare's Globe. *The Daily Express*, June 3, 2005, *Theatre Record* 21 (2005): 744 - 747.

Foucault, Michel. *Discipline and Punish: The Birth of the Prison*, trans. by Alan Sheridan. London: Penguin, 1977.

Gurr, Andrew. "Staging at the Globe". In *Shakespeare's Globe Rebuilt*. Edited by R. Mulryne and M. Shewring. Cambridge: Cambridge University Press, 1997.

Loehlin. James N. *Shakespeare in Performance: "Henry V"*. Manchester: Manchester University Press, 1996.

Macaulay, Alistair Review of Beaumont and Fletcher's *The Maid's Tragedy* and Middleton's *A Chaste Maid in Cheapside* in *The Financial Times*, August 30, 1997, *Theatre Record* 17 (1997): 1087.

Pearsall, Judy, ed. *The New Oxford Dictionary of English*. Oxford: Clarendon Press, 1998.

Samuel, Raphael. *Theatres of Memory: Vol 1: Past and Present in Contemporary Culture*. London: Verso, 1994.

Shakespeare, William. *The Oxford Shakespeare: The Complete Works*, 2nd edition. Edited by John Jowett, William Montgomery, Gary Taylor, and Stanley Wells, Oxford: Oxford University Press, 2005.

Thomson, Peter: 'The New Globe: Monument or Portent?' In *On Actors and Acting*. Exeter: Exeter University Press, 2003.

Tillyard, E. M. W. *The Elizabethan World Picture*. London: Chatto and Windus, 1950.

Weimann, Robert. *Author's Pen and Actor's Voice: Playing and Writing in Shakespeare's Theatre*. Edited by Helen Higbee and William West. Cambridge: Cambridge University Press, 2000.

Wiles, David. *A Short History of the Western Performance Space*, Cambridge and New York: 2003.

Worthen, W. B. "Reconstructing the Globe: Constructing Ourselves". *Shakespeare Survey* 52 (1999): pp. 33-45.

CHAPTER NINE

"EVER HOLY AND UNSTAINED": ILLUMINATING THE FEMINIST *CENCI* THROUGH MARY WOLLSTONECRAFT AND SHAKESPEARE'S *TITUS ANDRONICUS*

KRISTINE JOHANSAN

[The prevailing opinion is] that with chastity all is lost that is respectable in woman. Her character depends on the observance of one virtue, though the only passion fostered in her heart—is love. Nay, the honour of woman is not made even to depend on her will.
—Mary Wollstonecraft, *A Vindication of the Rights of Woman*[1]

A Vindication of the Rights of Woman was published in the same year Percy Bysshe Shelley was born, in 1792. Although he would develop ties of the closest kind to the offspring of the book's author, he would never, in fact, meet Mary Wollstonecraft. Like another inspiration to Shelley, Shakespeare, Wollstonecraft would inform the poet's art, would be a "lodestar" to him.[2] Evidence of this inspiration runs as a current through *The Cenci*, his 1819 tragedy which was deemed "the best play since the time of Shakespeare".[3] *The Cenci* dramatizes the story of the sixteenth-century Cenci family of Rome, who suffer under their patriarch's wickedness. The play's heroine, Beatrice Cenci, is raped by her father and, seeking revenge both for this act and for her father's determination to destroy her family, Beatrice, her step-mother, and her brother hire murderers to kill Cenci. When the act and plot are discovered, the Cenci are executed. It is a close reading with Shakespeare, with whom Shelley was "obsessed", that further illuminates a distinctly feminist quality to

---

[1] Wollstonecraft, *A Vindication of the Rights of Woman*, p. 92.
[2] Crompton, *Shelley's Dream Women*, p. 96.
[3] Bate, *Shakespeare and the English Romantic Imagination*, p. 206.

Shelley's drama and its victim-heroine.[4] *The Cenci* and the ordeal of its heroine, Beatrice, in particular parallel Shakespeare's *Titus Andronicus* and the tragic Lavinia. The value-system of both Romes, the prospect of death and shame, the problem of revenge and patriarchy—such themes bind both women across temporal lines, uniting them in ways beyond their victimhood. Underlying the suffering shared by these women is their society's assertion that a woman raped, "ruined", is a woman forever shamed and without value. That Titus ultimately murders his daughter to release her from her "shame" further solidifies this concept. Shelley's heroine also dies, but, in contrast, not before she revenges herself and declares her desire to live, even with the burden of remembering an incestuous rape. Such a presentation echoes Mary Wollstonecraft's argument that "[woman] was not created merely to be the solace of man, and the sexual should not destroy the human character".[5] With an exploration of *Titus Andronicus*, her arguments will be used to reveal the feminist nature of Shelley's *The Cenci,* a nature starkly absent from *Titus.*

The ideas of a woman's virtue and value within each respective play are firmly established in the opening scenes of both *Titus Andronicus* and *The Cenci.* Lavinia's first words are those of an obedient, expectant daughter who praises her "noble lord and father" and kneels before him, asking him to "bless [her] with [his] victorious hand"; Lavinia, in turn, is praised as "the cordial of [Titus's] age" and he wishes her to "outlive [her] father's days/And fame's eternal date, for virtue's praise" (I.i.158-68). That is, Lavinia's virtue is so exceptional that he prays she "live even longer than fame, which is supposed to live forever".[6] Similarly, Cardinal Camillo lauds Beatrice as Cenci's "gentle daughter" and "thinks her sweet looks, which make all things else/Beauteous and glad, might kill the fiend within [Cenci]".[7] Both Shakespeare and Shelley employ irony here to underscore the cruel fortunes of these women: Lavinia will not only die before her father, and at his hand, but her infamy will be in her "loss" of virtue, not its preservation;[8] similarly, Beatrice's celebrated virtue is used against her when her father—eager to corrupt her goodness—rapes her, thus empowering, not eradicating, "the fiend within" him.

---

[4] Ibid, p. 221.
[5] Wollstonecraft, *Vindication*, p.69.
[6] *Titus Andronicus*, ed. Jonathan Bate. See note on I.i.170-171.
[7] Shelley, *The Cenci*, I.i.43-5.
[8] I use inverted commas here to emphasise that Lavinia's society regarded the loss of chastity, in any form outside of wedlock, as a loss of virtue.

As the virtues of Lavinia and Beatrice are extolled, so too is their value—defined in the sense first of property, then of "worldly utility". *Titus'* opening scene reveals the status of Lavinia in Roman society: she is an item to be given by her father and an object of contest. Saturninus, "to advance/[Titus's] name and honourable family", will make Lavinia his empress; Titus, in gratitude, "consecrate[s]/[His] sword, [his] chariot, and [his] prisoners" (I.i.238-49). In essence, the men conduct a trade in show of thanks and honour of each other. Lavinia's status as property is fully underscored by the behaviour of Bassianus and her brothers; to Titus, Bassianus protests "[Lavinia] is mine" (I.i.276) and Marcus declares "*Suum cuique* [to each his own] is our Roman justice:/This prince in justice seizeth but his own", thereby employing a "technical legal term for taking possession of property" (I.i.280-1).[9] Lavinia's silence on the entire matter - she speaks when spoken to by Saturninus, and then to approve of his clemency towards Tamora and her sons - reflects her acceptance of these proprietal terms.[10] While Cenci's actions, his tyranny over his family, betray the idea of Beatrice's possessing a sub-human status within their household, it is her priest-friend Orsino who first muses on how he might avoid being "debarred from all access" to her.[11] He conjures images of Beatrice in animalistic terms: he will cast a "net/From which she shall not escape".[12] In Act IV Shelley gives Lucretia language that affirms the status of women: Cenci might "Pity [his] daughter; *give* her to some friend/In marriage: so that she may tempt [him] not/To hatred, or worse thoughts, if worse there be".[13]

Such conceptualising of women as property is inextricably tied to Wollstonecraft's argument that "in treating of morals, particularly when women are alluded to, writers have too often considered virtue in a very limited sense, and made the foundation of it solely *worldly utility*".[14] For if a man possesses a good, what use is that good to him if it is ruined, if something occurs to take its value from it? Rape, a "loss" of chastity and virtue beyond the control of the victim, is that which not only devalues Beatrice and Lavinia, but shames them in the natures of their rape: Beatrice's father is her rapist, and Lavinia was raped multiple times and then physically mutilated. She is thus rendered physically "useless"; Lavinia can no longer perform those domestic activities for which her

---

[9] See note in Bate, *Titus Andronicus,* on I.i.285
[10] I.i.270-272.
[11] *The Cenci*, I.ii.71.
[12] Ibid, I.ii.82-83.
[13] Ibid, 4.1.20-23. My italics.
[14] Wollstonecraft, *Vindication*, p.93. My italics.

family praises her: her lute-playing, her sewing with her "lily hands", her education of Lucius (2.4.44). As Catharine Stimpson writes, "The fact of having been raped obliterates all of a woman's previous claims to virtue. One *sexual* experience hereafter will define her".[15]

Shelley, following Wollstonecraft, deviates from this definition. Beatrice's rejection of the notion that her "wrong" defines her is most evident in her exit out of her trauma-induced madness. Beatrice refuses to allow her mental anguish to consume her; she will retain her "utility"; she will reject death; she will plot her father's murder. "Something must be done" she swears, and, "solemnly" - and matter-of-factly - she tells Orsino of what has happened: "a wrong so great and strange" that "is, and [that] has been; Advise me how it shall not be again".[16] These are the words of a woman who has "unravelled [her] entangled will", who has resolved to act: "to be brief and bold" in her revenge.[17] Like Wollstonecraft, Beatrice rejects the idea "that with [her] chastity all is lost"; the former does not equate personal "honour" with "chastity"—it is a "strange notion".[18] Ultimately, it is Beatrice's *action* against her father, and not her body as the locus of action, that will, in some sense, "define" her for history's annals.

That Beatrice rejects "self-murder" is a significant move away from her previous notions that "'twere wise to die",[19] a departure Lavinia does not, and cannot make,[20] and one that expresses a sensitivity again to the value of a woman "[in the respect that she possesses reasons] as a world in [her]self".[21] The argument for a woman's rationality and ability to reason is one that Wollstonecraft emphasises consistently through *A Vindication of the Rights of Woman*, and one that Shelley will make through Beatrice's language and action throughout *The Cenci*. It is her "subtle mind" that Orsino fears; it is she who reasons herself away from marriage to him; it is she who suspects "some dreadful ill/Must have befallen [her] brothers" when Cenci holds a feast in honour of them. It is she, too, whose reasonable arguments persuade Marzio and Cardinal Camillo to declare her and her family's innocence and it is she who exposes the injustice of

---

[15] Stimpson, "Shakespeare and the Soil of Rape", p. 62.
[16] *The Cenci*, III.i.139; III.i.146-147.
[17] *The Cenci*, III.i.220; III.i.228.
[18] Wollstonecraft, *Vindication*, p. 92.
[19] *The Cenci*, III.i.132, III.i.148, II.i.57.
[20] In her mutilated state, suicide would be literally impossible—see Demetrius' crude play on this in 2.4. Moreover, her inability to speak leaves the reader (but perhaps not the audience) at a disadvantage to know her thoughts.
[21] Wollstonecraft, *Vindication*, p.69.

the court: "Ha! Wilt thou be [my accuser],/Who art my judge? Accuser, witness, judge,/What, all in one?"[22] Finally, Beatrice's repeated declarations of innocence recall Lucretia's own insistence that Beatrice deserves "the peace of innocence" in her misery: it is a "crime, and punishment/By which [Beatrice] suffer[s]", and her mother vows "whate'er [she] may have suffered, [she] has done/No evil". So too does Beatrice believe in the "high and holy" nature of Cenci's murder, that "Earth and Heaven" are "consenting arbiters" in the act.[23]

Shelley's insistence upon Beatrice's innocence is a progressive rejection of the implication of a woman's guilt in her rape. But, as "rape in a shame culture makes women guilty", Lavinia suffers the consequence: her father kills her.[24] That Lavinia's culture is indeed one which equates rape with shame is evident before the rape occurs, in Lavinia's pleas to Tamora to "be a charitable murderer" and save her "from their worse-than-killing lust" by "tumbl[ing] [her] into some loathsome pit/Where never man's eye may behold [her] body" (II.iii.175-8). This last line implies that Lavinia's body has elicited this lust, and thus bears some guilt; she therefore wishes that it never be seen again. As Jonathan Bate observes, the line also "emphasizes 'man's eye': she will be ashamed to be seen, yet the men in the play will insist on displaying her".[25] Moreover, Shakespeare stresses her sense of shame further as, discovered by Marcus, she attempts to fly from him; he tells her family she was "seeking to hide herself, as doth the deer/That hath received some unrecuring wound" (III.i.89-90). Rather than survive multiple rapes and mutilation and the accompanying humiliation and internal pain, Lavinia sought to hide in the woods and die. Her rapist and even her father imply their preference of death to her current state: Chiron cruelly claims that "'Twere my cause I should go hang myself' (II.iv.9); Titus laments "he that wounded her/Hath hurt me more than had he killed me dead" (III.i.91-2). Titus exposes the depth of this "shame culture" by asking Saturninus's opinion of the story of Virginius. The Emperor concedes that Virginius was right to slay his "enforced, stained, and deflowered" daughter "because the girl should not survive her shame,/And by her presence still renew his sorrows" (V.iii.38-41). For these same reasons - "mighty, strong, effectual" (V.iii.42) - Titus murders his only daughter, whose shame dies with her (V.iii.45).

Thus Lavinia, like Beatrice, ultimately succumbs to the forces of her patriarchal society—a force Shelley, like Wollstonecraft, so determinedly

---

[22] *The Cenci*, V.iii.174-6.

[23] *The Cenci*, IV.iii.35; IV.iv.24.

[24] Stimpson, 'Shakespeare and the Soil of Rape', note 5, p. 63.

[25] Bate, ed., *Titus Andronicus*, note on II.ii.177.

wished to undermine. Repeatedly in *A Vindication of the Rights of Woman*, Wollstonecraft extols the importance of a woman's economic independence and derides the hereditary system of property in place in her time. Indeed, she did "not wish [women] to have power over men; but over themselves".[26] This is precisely the power Beatrice seeks in *The Cenci*: she rejects the idea of marriage to remain as the true protector of her family, thus usurping the role her tyrannical father should have filled; and, having her personal control literally raped of her by her father, she reclaims it through his murder. However, Beatrice's participation in revenge, like Lavinia's participation in the murder of her rapists, cannot erase the memory and self-knowledge of the rape. Nor does the knowledge of a "devilish wrong" alter the Pope's decree that "[The Cenci] must die"; in eradicating Beatrice and her conspirators, he eradicates a force which sought "to weaken the paternal power" which he held "of most dangerous example/[...] Being, as 'twere, the shadow of his own".[27] Yet even as Beatrice must hand over her life to her society, she does not believe that she must relinquish her legacy; Shelley allows her one last outlet to subvert tyrannical power. Beatrice instructs Bernardo to "be constant [...]] to the faith that I,/Tho' wrapt in a strange cloud of crime and shame,/Lived ever holy and unstained".[28]

What must be noted, before concluding, is the preface Shelley wrote to *The Cenci* and its seemingly contradictory sentiments to the feminist elements that are present in his drama. Shelley argues in his preface that:

> Undoubtedly, no person can be truly dishonoured by the act of another; and the fit return to make to the most enormous injuries is kindness and forbearance, and a resolution to convert the injurer from his dark passions by peace and love. Revenge, retaliation, atonement, are pernicious mistakes. If Beatrice had thought in this manner she would have been wiser and better; *but she would never have been a tragic character.*[29]

Thus Shelley the man reflects on Shelley the poet: dramatic necessity and the reality upon which he based his drama have informed his *Cenci*. His first statement, that "no person can be truly dishonoured" echoes in its embedded sentiments Wollstonecraft's belief that "the sexual should not destroy the human character".[30] But Shelley's preface ultimately turns

---

[26] Wollstonecraft, *Vindication*, p. 81
[27] *The Cenci*, V.iv.14; II.ii.54-6.
[28] *The Cenci*, V.iv.146-149.
[29] Ibid, preface, 4.
[30] Wollstonecraft, *Vindication*, p. 69.

away from Wollstonecraft in his failure to demand an outlet of justice for the victims of "enormous injuries" in arguing for a response of "kindness and forebearance". Because her patriarchal society failed to protect her from her father-rapist, Beatrice resorted to violence. Shelley the man, rather than Shelley the poet, would have believed that Beatrice could survive her trauma without turning to murder. Her *human* character was rational and strong enough to endure such violence. But as Shelley notes, had she responded with peace and love—which, admittedly, would not reflect the most human of sentiments, but rather the most sanctimonious— she would not have been a character to appeal to the hearts of her audience. Ultimately, the contradiction evident in the preface is the contradiction of man and poet. As Anne Wroe, Shelley's latest biographer, has stated, "the poet and the man are of two different natures; two universes kept apart".[31]

"[The prevailing opinion is] that with chastity all is lost that is respectable in woman. Her character depends on the observance of one virtue, though the only passion fostered in her heart—is love. Nay, the honour of woman is not made even to depend on her will."[32] In citing again this essay's epigraph, I reiterate Wollstonecraft's rejection of her time's "prevailing opinion". Wollstonecraft's observation points to the seeming humiliation that the will and love of a woman have no bearing on society's opinion of her honour; a woman's chastity alone determines her character. Ultimately, *The Cenci* rejects the ideology Wollstonecraft questioned in 1792 and that still persisted during Shelley's life. In Beatrice Cenci, Shelley crafted a woman who, like Wollstonecraft, acts against the social dictates of her time. The feminist qualities of Shelley's tragedy are illuminated further when paralleled with Shakespeare's *Titus Andronicus*: reading Beatrice and Lavinia together highlights the extent to which Lavinia becomes a pitiable, tragic character created and destroyed by the proprietal patriarchal system of her society. Lavinia becomes, in opposition to Beatrice, a sacrifice rather than a martyr in search of justice. The contrasts between *Titus* and *The Cenci* reveal the latter's commitment to several of *Vindication's* ideals. Indeed, by the end of the play Beatrice's honour is bound to her unflappable belief both in her and her family's innocence and in her attempt to right an "unnatural" wrong. She suffers tremendously, but Shelley creates her again as the pillar of her family; her presentation as a reasonable, intelligent woman echoes Wollstonecraft's own firm belief in a woman's rationality; and finally, her actions attack a

---

[31] From her "Searching for Shelley" lecture given at the University of St Andrews, 21 April 2006.
[32] Wollstonecraft, *Vindication*, p. 92.

patriarchal society that has failed her, much as Wollstonecraft herself attacked her own from the pages of *Vindication* and her other writings.

Works Cited

Bate, Jonathan. *Shakespeare and the English Romantic Imagination.* Oxford: Clarendon Press, 1986.

Crompton, Margaret. *Shelley's Dream Women.* London: Cassell & Company, Ltd, 1967.

Shakespeare, William. *Titus Andronicus*, ed. Jonathan Bate. London: Routledge, 1995.

—. The Oxford *Complete Works*, gen. eds. Stanley Wells and Gary Taylor, et al. Oxford: Clarendon Press, 1988.

Shelley, Percy Bysshe. *The Cenci.* London: Reeves & Turner, 1886.

Stimpson, Catharine R. "Shakespeare and the Soil of Rape". *The Woman's Part: Feminist Criticism of Shakespeare*, eds. Carolyn Ruth Swift Lenz, Gayle Greene, and Carol Thomas Neely. Urbana: Univ. of Illinois Press, 1980.

Wollstonecraft, Mary. *A Vindication of the Rights of Woman*, ed. Miriam Brody. London: Penguin Books, 2004.

CHAPTER TEN

NARCISSUS AND MODERNITY
IN *SHAKESPEARE'S SONNETS*

WILL MCKENZIE

In *Shakespeare's Perjured Eye* Joel Fineman reads *Shakespeare's Sonnets* in broadly Lacanian terms. Fineman thinks that the "modernity" of the *Sonnets* is due to the way their structure corresponds to the "modern" structure of subjectivity discovered by Lacanian psychoanalysis. The "young man" and dark lady sub-sequences correspond to the Imaginary and the Symbolic respectively, which by extension associates the "young man" sonnets with narcissism and the dark lady sonnets with modernity. In this essay, I argue that this structure, which I describe as the "difference between dichotomy and difference", fails to assimilate narcissism with modernity sufficiently. Drawing on Julia Kristeva's revision of Lacanian theory, especially her revision of his theory of narcissism, I read the *Sonnets* instead in terms of an "oscillation between dichotomy and difference". I set out how this "oscillatory principle" works with reference to some of the *Sonnets'* broader themes, narrative strands, and use of language. I then establish a link between this "oscillatory principle" and the elements of Kristevan theory which connect narcissism with modernity. I conclude by exploring how the relationship between narcissism and modernity oscillates within the space of a single poem, namely sonnet 24.

I argue for this "oscillatory principle" because I think it theorises the *Sonnets'* impact for our time, revealing how these poems reflect upon an increasingly narcissistic modernity. Julia Kristeva says that Narcissus is still a "modern character", even though Narcissus was "already very old"

when Ovid rewrote his story two thousand years ago.[1] Themes and images
from Ovid's tale still seem pertinent to cultural concerns in modern, high-
capitalist Western societies. Narcissus is tempted, seduced and deceived
by his reflection; the modern Narcissus is in turn tempted, seduced and
deceived by a continual bombardment of images. Narcissus is vain, in the
sense of futility and of superficiality; latest debt-figures reveal a modern
Narcissus addicted to exciting but ultimately insubstantial consumerism.[2]
Narcissus is solipsistic; the modern Narcissus is plugged into the Matrix,
addicted to the comforting but melancholy virtual contact of the chat-
room. Narcissus is empty, unfulfilled: the boy he loves is a mere image.
The modern Narcissus emotes and identifies through virtual images and
carefully-arranged publicity events, found in magazines like *Heat* and
Closer, as much as through direct personal contact. The sheer outpouring
of grief that followed the death Princess Diana is a vivid and still fairly
recent example of the phenomenon. It would not be unreasonable to think
that, for some of her millions of mourners, Diana's death was a more
intense and "real" experience than any family bereavement.

Kristeva's observation that Narcissus is modern encourages a rethink
of the relationship between Shakespeare's use of Narcissus,
Shakespearean modernity and the periodising term "early modern". Hugh
Grady observes: "[o]ne of the many remarkable features of the [...]
archive of writings about [...] Shakespeare is the frequency with which
his work is termed 'modern'".[3] Shakespeare is often supposed to have
anticipated the modernity we live in. Perhaps he even invented it.
Fineman's *Shakespeare's Perjured Eye,* the "most brilliant, original study
of the *Sonnets* of the last twenty-five years, if not of all time" believes in
just such an invention.[4] "[I]n his sonnets Shakespeare invents a [...] new

---

[1] Kristeva, *Tales of Love*, p. 121; Shepherdson, "Telling Tales of Love:
Philosophy, Literature, and Psychoanalysis", p. 96.

[2] On Saturday 5 May 2007 Ashley Seager in the *Guardian* noted: "The Insolvency
Service reported that a total of 30,075 people went bankrupt or took out an
individual voluntary arrangement (IVA) between January and March. That marked
an increase of 1.2% over the previous quarter and a hefty 24% from the same
period last year". The article goes on to say that mortgages taken out in a booming
property market make up the bulk of personal debt in Britain, but consumer credit
or "unsecured loans", still make up £200 billion of the money owed by Britons
today.

[3] Grady, 'Introduction: Shakespeare and modernity' in *Shakespeare and
Modernity: Early modern to millennium*, p. 1.

[4] This praise for Fineman is found in Schiffer, *Shakespeare's Sonnets: Critical
Essays*, p. 40.

poetic subjectivity".[5] The connection between this "new" poetic subjectivity and modernity is not merely implicit. Fineman later suggests that "Shakespeare marks the beginning of the modernist self".[6] His point should not be obscured by the quibbling difference between "modern" as socio-historical category and "modernist" as literary category. *Shakespeare's Sonnets* inaugurate an entire "epoch of subjectivity".[7] For Fineman, Shakespeare invented something four hundred years ago which has not yet been wholly superseded. We moderns still occupy the epoch Shakespeare invented, or at least its very recent and very close relation. Our modernity still bears its marks.

I share Fineman's commitment to the continuing and urgent relevance of *Shakespeare's Sonnets*, but suggest that his brilliant reading of Shakespearean modernity obscures modernity's vital and contemporary connection with Narcissus and narcissism. This is partly due to Fineman's use of Lacanian theory. Lacan's model of subjectivity is Fineman's representative of modernity, the constant against which the modern subjectivity of *Shakespeare's Sonnets* may be tested. Lacan's key principle is that subjectivity is language, and language is lack. Humans speak because they need things, and they need things because they lack them. Language is caused by lack but there is also a lack inherent in language. Anyone grappling with a foreign language will realise that language lacks any direct, logical connection between the properties of a word and the properties of the thing indicated by that word. Lacan says that life prior to full consciousness is largely free from language, so it is also largely free from the lack associated with it. It is thus pre-subjective. Language is neither acquired nor necessary because the baby's bodily needs are sufficiently fulfilled by the maternal body. This pre-subjective experience is called the Imaginary and it is narcissistic because it is marked by the "mirror stage". The infant's mirror-image gives it a sense of bodily coherence and fullness to cope with the chaotic mix of sensations perceived in its young body. By contrast, Lacan's Symbolic, his name for the psyche's ability to organise experience into structures of meaning, is post-subjective. It is created by language and lack. According to Lacan, we keep speaking because we keep lacking, needing and wanting things – the famous Lacanian "desire" – but most of the time we are not conscious of this. Fineman says Shakespeare's dark lady sonnets

---

[5] Fineman, *Shakespeare's Perjured Eye: The Invention of Poetic Subjectivity in the Sonnets,* p. 1.
[6] Fineman, *Shakespeare's Perjured Eye*, p. 47.
[7] Fineman, *Shakespeare's Perjured Eye*, p. 47.

are acutely and anxiously aware of the disparity of words and things so they anticipate Lacan's insights regarding language and its underlying framework of lack. This is what makes them modern. Narcissism is therefore associated with the Imaginary and pre-subjectivity, and modernity is associated with language, subjectivity and the Symbolic. Narcissism and modernity are implicitly segregated.

This Lacanian segregation of narcissism from modernity - what might be called Fineman's "blind-spot" - is also, and obviously more substantially, due to Fineman's early death in 1989. Fineman's Lacanian modernity is no longer ours. Had he lived, it is likely Fineman would have revised his work to take issue with the increasingly visible connection between narcissism and modernity, and brought narcissism and modernity together within the over-arching structure he envisaged for *Shakespeare's Sonnets* as a whole. Fineman argues that the "young man" and dark lady sub-sequences interlock. They are "cross-coupled". They relate to each other like fairness and foulness in the chant from *Macbeth*: "[f]air is foul and foul is fair" (I.i.10). Let us try to see how Fineman's segregation of narcissism and modernity operates within this "cross-coupled" system. Appropriately, Fineman uses a "cross-coupler" to describe this system: "[t]he first sub-sequence tends to derive similarity out of difference, the second instead tends to derive difference out of similarity".[8] Fineman's analysis of sonnets 46 and 47 shows how the "young man" sonnets derive similarity out of difference. The "eye" and "heart" are "at a mortal war" in 46 but do "good turns now unto the other" in 47. Fineman argues that this war or peace is immaterial, and that the "eye" and "heart" are only superficially different: "[w]hat these two young man poems share [...] thematically and formally, is the sameness of their differences, what joins them together is a structural identity [...] that is yet more fundamental and more powerful than their apparent opposition".[9] The "dark lady" sonnets, by contrast, lack this "structural identity". Fineman argues that their particular insights into the "languageness of language" prevent the harmonisation of dichotomous opposites. Quoting "when my love swears that she is made of truth,/I do believe her, though I know she lies" (from sonnet 138) and "mine eyes seeing this, say this is not" (from sonnet 137), Fineman notes that "[t]he dark lady sonnets differ from the young man sonnets because they articulate thematically the paradoxical duplicity of a language which is verbal, not visual".[10] The "dark lady" poems "derive

---

[8] *Shakespeare's Perjured Eye*, p.74.
[9] *Shakespeare's Perjured Eye*, pp. 73-74.
[10] *Shakespeare's Perjured Eye*, p. 243.

difference out of similarity" (rather than "similarity out of difference"),
because the difference being articulated is not between two reconcilable
things, such as an "eye" or "heart", but between one level of language and
another. For Fineman, the novelty and modernity of the "dark lady" poems
lies in the way they apply the logical, epistemological antinomy of the
"Cretan" liar-paradox to passion, to feelings of love and lust. The "I" that
"believe[s] her" must logically be different to the "I" that "know[s] she
lies". The worrying aspect of these sentences is that they are able to
describe genuine, eroticised subjectivity despite their grammatical illogic.
The internalised difference articulated in the "dark lady" sonnets, and their
presentment of contradictory relationships between what is being said and
how it is said, anticipate the Lacanian insight that subjectivity is premised
on language and language is premised on lack. For Fineman, they
therefore invent a new subjectivity and predict Lacanian modernity.

If the "young man" sonnets are underpinned by "structural identity",
and the "dark lady" sonnets are not, then this may be rephrased as follows:
the "young man" sonnets are characterised by relations of dichotomy and
the "dark lady" sonnets by relations of difference. Dichotomy is less
complex and troubling than difference because it is more symmetrical.
According to the logic of Fineman's "structural identity", one element in a
dichotomous relationship is precisely opposite to the other. It therefore
follows that each property of the first element has to relate in the same
dichotomous way with each property of the second. Dichotomy is thus
defined according to a transcendental, ordering, harmonising logic which
recognises dichotomy as such. This logic dissects the two dichotomous
objects into a common and measurable set of properties, and then ticks
these properties off one by one as dichotomous.

Reminiscent of the relative harmony and contentment of the Lacanian
Imaginary, the narcissistic "young man" poems, marked by "stuctural
identity" and relations of dichotomy, are more harmonious than the
modern "dark lady" poems, whose disharmonious relations of difference
recall instead the "modern" subjectivity diagnosed by the Lacanian
Symbolic. The difference between the "young man" and "dark lady" sub-
sequences is therefore the difference between dichotomy and difference.
The difference between dichotomy and difference and the segregation
between narcissism and modernity both remain constant despite the many
other kinds of connections Fineman makes between the "cross-coupled"
sub-sequences.[11] There is, therefore, a parallel and correspondence

---

[11] Fineman's "cross-coupled" relationship, by definition, suggests that the two sub-
sequences share similarities as well as differences; for example, both sub-

between Fineman's difference between dichotomy and difference and his segregation of narcissism from modernity. If Fineman's difference between dichotomy and difference may be challenged and nuanced, then, so its parallel – the segregation of narcissism from modernity – may potentially be challenged as well.

This is why I disagree with Fineman's principle of difference between dichotomy and difference, and why I believe instead that *Shakespeare's Sonnets* operate according to a principle of *oscillation* between dichotomy and difference. For Fineman, the movement from disharmony to harmony characterises the "young man" poems and differentiates them from the "dark lady" poems. For me, there is a continual movement from harmony to disharmony and back again, and this is an additional continuity from the "young man" sonnets to the "dark lady" sonnets. This oscillatory principle is common to both sub-sequences, strengthening their cross-coupled relationship.

The key characteristics of the oscillatory principle are as follows: beauty oscillates to and from the bodies of the protagonists. Multiple sensations of time fall into harmony and away again. The poet's opinion of his own poetry oscillates between abject futility and vainglorious arrogance, depending on varying perceptions of what words may do and what they may not do. The oscillatory movement is continually powered by the perception of one element of the dichotomy in relation to the other, by the memory or the projection of its opposite. Harmony is only perceptible in relation to the whirl of change that surrounds it diachronically and synchronically. Fineman's "structural identity", the conceptual basis for the association of narcissism with dichotomy, and therefore narcissism's estrangement from modernity, is troubled, continually, by the remainder or reminder of difference.

Sonnet 52 contains some free-flowing variations on this principle: "Therefore are feasts so solemn and so rare/Since, seldom coming, in the long year set/Like stones of worth they thinly placed are,/Or captain jewels in the carcanet" (lines 5-8). The poet does not simply note the tension between deferred pleasure and actual pleasure in his description of "solemn, rare feasts", he implies that this tension changes in the poet's consciousness as time goes on. Sonnet 60 applies the idea to the natural world, stressing the waves' eternal tension between togetherness and distance, an apparent reference to Ovid's philosophy of *perpetuum mobile*: "Like as the waves make towards the pebbled shore,/So do our

---

sequences "question their praise"; both also exhibit a degree of literary self-consciousness (See *Shakespeare's Perjured Eye*, p.159).

minutes hasten to their end,/Each changing place with that which went before,/In sequent toil all forwards do contend" (lines 1-4).

Sonnet 56 applies the idea to the circling seasons, to absence and reunion, to hunger and fulfilment, and, most importantly, to love itself. "Sweet love, renew thy force. Be it not said/Thy edge should blunter be than appetite,/Which but today by feeding is allayed,/Tomorrow sharpened in his former might" (lines 1-4). Sonnet 62, the most obviously narcissistic of the sonnets, ("Sin of self-love possesseth all mine eye") concludes by bringing "young man" and poet together, in just the kind of dichotomous-harmonious relationship Fineman deems typical of the "young man" sonnets. "'Tis thee, my self, that for myself I praise,/Painting my age with beauty of thy days". Yet the equilibrium suggested by the repeated word "myself" and the implicit dichotomy at work in the contrast of "age" and "beauty" seem to be troubled by the present participle in the final line. The poet stresses he is still "painting" – he will presumably always be painting – rather than saying "I have painted" which would conclude the poem in permanent harmony and love. Even if the continued act of "painting" is a conclusion of sorts, "painting" implies continued effort is necessary to keep this harmony in place. The inevitable natural drift of time is continually liable to separate lover from beloved.

The oscillatory principle is especially strong in the procreation sonnets. The young man's narcissism – he is, famously, "contracted to his own bright eyes" (sonnet 1, line 5) – only serves to accentuate and emphasise the oscillations between beauty and physical matter. The young man's current beauty will disappear, but it will rise into his son precisely as it does so. This dialogue between beauty and individual human lives will only continue if the young man's unique beauty is perpetuated in the form of a child. One quantity falls in fairly precise direct proportion to the rise in the other. Beauty and human lives are like alternate waves on Shakespeare's pebbled shore, each "changing place with that which goes before" (sonnet 60, line 3).

This idea is developed in the poems which trope the narcissistic young man with a rose, one of the most persistent image-associations in the sequence (see sonnets 94 and 95 for example). The rose's property of "beauty" only temporarily coincides with its physical matter. Then it turns into "canker". This materialised image of the young man's dubious ethics, where excess must be constantly monitored and managed, also applies to the poems' more general anatomical theory of the individual body. Sonnets 44 and 45 present the body as a continuing oscillation of harmony and disharmony between air, water, earth and fire. Sonnets 118 and 119 suggest that corporeal harmony is paradoxically restored by poison. The "dark lady" sonnet 129 applies the principle to the more sexually-suggestive saving and expenditure of "spirit".

The *Sonnets'* portrayal of beauty and decay or pleasure and pain continually flowing in and out of the individual body resembles Lacan's theoretical dynamic of language. Language lacks any ontological oneness with the sense-data it represents, so meaning is generated instead when signifiers interrelate, connect and clash with one another, when they oscillate with one another. Yet Shakespeare's silent but powerful juxtaposition of body and language represents an important modification to Fineman's Lacanian argument, which largely differentiates the dark lady sonnets from the "young man" sonnets on the basis of "languageness of language" and echoes Lacan's abstraction of the linguistic processes of the Symbolic from the bodily processes of the Imaginary. In the *Sonnets*, by contrast, the body often works like language, and language often works like the body. This cross-coupled relationship is, moreover, common to both "young man" and dark lady sequences.

The cross-coupling of the body and language may thus be argued to anticipate a theoretical system of modernity, modern subjectivity, and narcissism that supersedes Lacan's and talks more to our here and now. Following a Freudian and Lacanian tradition, Julia Kristeva holds that narcissism originates in very early life and stays with us in varying quantities and qualities as life goes on. Indeed, she stresses the need for a successfully-managed narcissism as well as the danger of its excesses. Her crucial innovation, however, is that an element of language, a signifying process, a modality of communicative practice begins in the Imaginary and survives into the Symbolic. This is a genuine departure from the Lacanian model which segregates Imaginary from the Symbolic on the basis of language, which holds that the subject is a subject precisely because s/he can speak, and that only the Symbolic may talk. In powerful contrast, Kristeva suggests that the Imaginary and the Symbolic are present and together in all speech. Speech therefore oscillates between Imaginary narcissistic "dichotomy" and Symbolic, modern "difference". Shakespeare's continual, silent suggestion of a language-like dynamic in the body is therefore consistent with Kristeva's contemporary observations. Kristeva suggests that the infant's body speaks in the Imaginary through the "semiotic" aspect of language. The "semiotic" may be defined as the manifestation of drives - the need to reach physical satisfaction - in communicative activity. It pertains, for example, to melody of intonation or tone of voice: the meaning of words that are not those words themselves. The other signifying practice, the "symbolic", more or less conforms to its Lacanian namesake. It refers to extra-subjective reality, interpreting that reality into discrete objects and organising it conceptually. Kristeva insists that each and every speech-act is spoken through the "semiotic" and the "symbolic". There is never one without the other, indeed, they are both necessary. Problems arise when there is a serious imbalance between them.

This is because such imbalances cause narcissism in various forms. That is to say, these imbalances characterise and are characterised by narcissistic phenomena in modern societies. Note, then, that Kristeva equates narcissism with disharmony rather than harmony. For example, speech characterised by an excess of the "symbolic" is polite and precise, but it has no real meaning for the speaker, nor for the surrounding world. It is therefore melancholy, nihilistic and solipsistic. No communication or continuity takes place. Speech characterised by the excess of the "semiotic", by contrast, is regressive echolalia or babbling. Resisting narcissism on one side or the other thus requires constant effort, a continual balancing-act of the symbolic and semiotic in real time. The Kristevan subject is a speaking subject, a subject-in-process. It only exists because it speaks, and it speaks in the real world.

Kristeva's recent topic is the subject's weakening resistance to the narcissism that results when either the "semiotic" or the "symbolic" hold a disproportionate sway over discourse. She argues that modern socio-cultural institutions are insufficient to the task of helping individual subjects maintain this resistance. "[S]ocial relations are indirectly lived through a representation" and market consumerism "valorise[s] appearance over substance, market value over the intrinsic value of the thing produced".[12] The spectacle, narcissistic in its excessive visuality and in its confusion of values, is Kristeva's most pressing concern today.[13] In the reading of sonnet 24 which follows, I argue that a comparable dynamic is articulated within the space of an individual sonnet. This sonnet tells a story where "modern" relations of difference move towards "narcissistic" relations of dichotomy and back again. The energy that propels that movement is comparable to the Kristevan tensions between

---

[12] Lechte, "The Imaginary and the Spectacle: Kristeva's View" in *Julia Kristeva: Live Theory*, p. 116.

[13] 'There are few works published since 1993 [...] where Kristeva does not make some reference to the society of the spectacle', Lechte, 'The Imaginary and the Spectacle', 117. Kristeva herself notes, 'this empire of the spectacle, when linked to other social problems, leads to what I have called, "new maladies of the soul"' (Julia Kristeva, quoted in Lechte, 'The Imaginary and the Spectacle', 117).

"semiotic" and "symbolic" modes of discourse, the modern struggle to manage narcissism within the language we use to connect with the world.

The oscillatory principle in practice: sonnet 24

Sonnet 24, I argue, offers a good example of the oscillatory principle within an individual sonnet because its story moves from relations of difference to a relation of dichotomy and back again. The opening lines immediately create relations of difference with their compressed and polyvalent language. "Mine eye hath *played* the painter, and hath steeled/Thy beauty's form in table of my heart" (my italics). The verb "played" - especially in Shakespeare - implies acting and theatre. The semantic association constructed between the "eye" and the "painter" is therefore far from solid or synonymous. On one hand, the poet's "eye" is only "playing" the "painter". On the other, the "painter" is only one role the "eye" might "play". The ambiguity caused by playing and painting is developed by a neo-platonic overtone. The painting eye is not painting the beloved's beauty but the "form" of that beauty, suggesting that the image created by the poet's "eye" exists beyond the material world. Within this ambiguous space, the kind of seeing being described might incorporate a form of imaginative or intuitive recollection, as well as the reception of purely visual images. The painting eye's spiritualising and aesthetic energies create something closer to an emotional or imaginatively recollected ideal.

When these factors are taken in combination, the clear suggestion is that the act of seeing is far from uniform. As the "eye" is playing some kind of role - "the painter" - it is unsure whether the eye passively observes concrete reality or actively creates its own reality. The act of seeing is differentiated from itself. The same may be said of the erotic, emotional sensation described in the first quatrain as a whole. This sensation is not single or unified. Rather than touching the whole person at once, it is presented as a drawn-out sequence of different stages. It touches in turn the "eye", the "heart" and the "body".

As well as being differentiated from each other, the "heart" and the "body" are each differentiated from themselves. The "form" of the beloved's beauty is not "steeled" in the heart itself, but "in table of my heart". This line may suggest that the poet's heart is purely and simply like a table-book. It may also suggest that the information received via the eye has transformed the heart into a table-book. Yet the paradox is that the specification of "table of my heart", being so precise, implies that that the heart has other, different properties and attributes. The implication is that the "heart" can act as a "table" but not just as a "table". A difference is therefore suggested between the heart's ability to act as a passive receptacle and its unspecified other abilities. The poet's "body" is differentiated from itself in a similar way. Continuing the painterly imagery from the first line, the body is a "frame". While the painterly imagery perhaps invokes the beloved's beauty, the image of the "body's frame", also invokes the image of the skeleton, a soulless, hollow space, devoid of and distinct from the conventional or contemporary notions of animism or humoral energies that mark the portrayal of the body in other sonnets.

Sonnet 24's opening quatrain is therefore, I argue, marked by relations of difference. Erotic experience is presented as a sequence of different stages, rather than a solitary, unified moment. The beloved's image is incorporated by turns into the poet's eye, heart and body. Even this simple concatenation is contested and complicated. This is because the poet does not simply talk about the "eye", "heart", or "body". He always complicates his descriptions with an image or comparison. The eye "play[s] the painter", the heart becomes "table of my heart" and the body becomes a "frame". The images' transformational qualities render these things different from themselves. Such relations of difference, I argue, run counter to the relations of dichotomy associated with Fineman's principle of "structural identity". The poem's opening therefore contains elements which potentially threaten the harmonious togetherness the poet desires with his beloved.

These movements and transitions between dichotomy and difference here are reflected by the semantic variations of "perspective", one of the poem's central conceits ("perspective it is best painter's art", line 4). If "perspective" is understood as the compositional arrangement of a painting, it may also be understood as a principle of "structural identity", ordering and aligning relations of difference, like those suggested in the first quatrain, into a relationship of dichotomy. The vanishing-point of a painting usually positions the viewer directly opposite that painting. The sonnet juxtaposes such a spatial relationship with a relationship of reciprocated emotional understanding. Yet "Perspective" also recalls another, anamorphic sense of "perspective" which distorts or misaligns acts of looking. Such images "rightly gazed upon,/Show nothing but confusion; eyed awry,/Distinguish form", as Bushy laments in *Richard II* (II.ii.18-20). They transform relations of dichotomy to relations of difference.

The idealised relationship of dichotomy described in the second quatrain thus seems troubled by relations of difference alluded to in the first. This may explain the urging, even anxious plea in lines five and six: "For through the painter *must* you see his skill/To find where your true image pictured lies" (my italics). "Painter" here refers back to the poet's "eye", recalling the first line's strong association between looking and painting. The plea is to take one form of perspective over another, to choose the symmetrical relation of dichotomy over the asymmetrical relation of difference. The beloved may thus see himself reflected "through" the glassy surface of the poet's eyes when poet and beloved face each other, just so a viewer may look "through" the surface of a canvas to make sense of the elements of a painting.

When poet and beloved turn and face each other in lines eight to ten, there is a genuine passage from a relation of difference to a relation of dichotomy. In line seven, the beloved's image is "hanging still" in the poet's "bosom's shop", invoking perhaps a sense of impatience and inertia. The following line, however, presents the beloved's gaze as a kind of magic ingredient. As well as awakening the "still" image, the reciprocal gaze brings the poet's internalised differences into a unified "perspective". This gaze smoothes away distortion and difference and creates a true, harmonious perspective of mutual reciprocation as the poem moves from the octave into the sestet.

If these claims seem exaggerated, let us look at the lines immediately following, lines nine and ten, which I see as the poem's central portrayal of the dichotomous relationship: "Now see what good turns eyes for eyes have done:/Mine eyes have drawn thy shape, and thine for me". Line nine's opening word "now" makes a clear break from the past in which the first, more tentative and ambiguous quatrains were written. It also recalls Fineman's dynamic where relations of dichotomy create similarity out of difference: the solitary moment ("now") brings different timeframes together. The amorous experience recounted by the writing, the writing itself, and our reading of that writing are all represented by this "now" to an equal degree of accuracy. This conciliation of timeframes is assimilated with other conciliations. Themes of intertwining reciprocity, love, trust, and togetherness are powerfully reinforced by certain formal features, such as repetitions of certain words within the line ("eyes for eyes") and of certain phonemes within the words ("*th*y shape, and *th*ine for me"). The poet's and beloved's reciprocal "drawing" presents a new and more harmonious context for the poem's painterly imagery. When the poet's eyes "draw" the beloved, they endow "beauty's form" with a definite "shape". Likewise, the first quatrain's divisions of the poet into "eye" "heart" and "body" are unified into a singular "shape" in and by the beloved's eyes.

Another connotation of "draw" develops the sense of a fully-achieved reciprocal relationship. As well as a synonym for "depict", "draw" may also be understood as a way of saying "extract" or "pull back". This different, more recursive meaning evokes the image of the poet and the beloved being reflected not just once in each others' eyes, but also being replicated within the eyes of each successive reflection. The reciprocal and symmetrical relationship thus recurs again and again, "drawing" progressively further back along the depth-lines of "perspective", towards an ever-decreasing vanishing point of ever-increasing intimacy.

The description of this "mutual render" (see sonnet 125, line 12) continues to the latter lines of the third quatrain. The beloved's eyes "[a]re windows to my breast, wherethrough the sun/Delights to peep, to gaze therein on thee". Yet while these lines continue the triumphant description of the lovers' reconciliation, there is no longer such a perfect coincidence between content and form. For example, the powerful run of monosyllables in the earlier lines is broken by the two-syllable words "windows", "wherethrough" "delights" and "therein". I am not trying to say here that monosyllabic words – which to some degree unify rhythmical pulse with the relay of information – automatically assume some form of magical unity between human beings, but in this context, their deployment had symbolised and strengthened the relationship of dichotomy. In doing away with them, these subsequent lines witness a new but almost entirely hidden tension between sound and sense. They subtly imply a movement away from relations of dichotomy and back towards relations of difference. Moreover, these faint but perceptible rhythmical modulations suggest that relations of dichotomy are inherently vulnerable to the inevitable progression of time. Were the use of monosyllabic words to continue, they would eventually cease to feel like symbols of dichotomous unity, and would start to feel repetitive, even oppressive. As well as benefiting the poem aesthetically, then, this introduction of more varied rhythms also suggests that perfect dichotomy cannot last forever. The integration of word and syllable with the integration of poet and beloved cannot be sustained: it would eventually cease to feel like bliss and start to feel like repression.

The themes of happiness and unity conceal the rhythmical transitions in the latter part of the quatrain. This subtle movement away from a relation of dichotomy and toward relations of difference, however, seems to anticipate the final couplet. The couplet conclusively rejects the mutual gaze of the poet and the beloved, on the basis that "the heart" is not fully taken into account. "Yet eyes this cunning want to grace their art:/They draw but what they see, know not the heart". Note that "draw" in line fourteen is an ironic and dismissive echo of "drawn" in line ten. This link is strengthened through the comparable wordplay of "draw" as "depict" and "draw" as "extract". As the eyes "draw but what they see", they are able to depict the beloved's outward form but unable to extract his "heart", his essence or his love. The couplet retrospectively laments that the relationship in lines nine and ten was not, in fact, the harmonious unity it appeared to be. The couplet is therefore uttered from a position of difference, which is all the more tragic by being compared belatedly with a relation of dichotomy.

I have hoped to show that sonnet 24 oscillates between relations of difference, to a relation of dichotomy, and then back again. The first quatrain portrays the amorous encounter as a differentiated sequence. These relations of difference are gradually worked away, and lines nine and ten portray a powerful relation of dichotomy, an image of harmony and togetherness. The couplet, however, exposes this relation of dichotomy as false: it fails to "know the heart". The poet thus finds himself at the close adrift and estranged from his beloved, and therefore back in a relation of difference.

This simple, oscillatory narrative is, I argue, propelled by an energy which characterises the Shakespearean persona throughout these sonnets. This persona continuously experiences his relationship with his beloved as some form of transition between relationships of dichotomy and difference. The poet's reflection on his changing position also actually effects a change in this position. This movement is apparent, for example, in the early anxiety surrounding "perspective". "Perspective" is potentially a metaphor for distortion and difference, but the poet refashions it into a structuring principle that can arrange differentiated elements into some form of harmony or order. "Perspective" thus becomes a powerful and enabling trope for the moment of harmony and togetherness when poet and beloved look at each others eyes. On the other hand, however, the rhythm of the sonnet reveals a converse transition from dichotomy to difference. The monosyllables that phonetically replicate the unity between poet and beloved give way to a more varied rhythm, thus avoiding the dull and claustrophobic monotony which any unified, dichotomous relationship threatens to become.

These examples reveal a constant undertow in the *Sonnets*. The very act of articulating one form of relationship moves it towards the other one. The poet continually adapts to the difference between the now-moment and the now-just-passed, displaying and presupposing an acute awareness of the difference between "now" and "then", a difference crucial to any perception of modernity. It is perhaps worth noting at this point that sonnet 24 also clearly takes up key motifs from Ovid's Echo-Narcissus story (*Metamorphoses* 3.339-510), such as the crucial but difficult difference between image and reality, the reciprocal, reflective image and its potential dangers. Sonnet 24's oscillatory narrative implies that narcissism is fascinating and repulsive, deadly and necessary by turns. It thus displays an uncanny grasp of the modern, narcissistic problematic, as diagnosed by Kristeva, not least in the way the problematic intersects with distinctive uses of rhythm and meaning in language. It is therefore a shame that this alert, "resistant" Shakespearean language seems smothered or censored by this narcissistic society of the spectacle. *Shakespeare in Love* and the more recent *Shakespeare Re-told*, for example, benefit from the cultural prestige of "Shakespeare". But they have reduced, or forgotten entirely, the language that makes Shakespeare Shakespeare in the first place. Thus making "Shakespeare" a marketable brand like any other, these ventures have sadly reduced him to the samey sameness of our modernity, and made him an element of the modern narcissism his language observes and contests.

Works Cited

Fineman, Joel. *Shakespeare's Perjured Eye: The Invention of Poetic Subjectivity in the Sonnets*. Berkeley, Los Angeles, London: University of California Press, 1986.

Grady, Hugh, ed. *Shakespeare and Modernity: Early Modern to Millennium Accents on Shakespeare*. London and New York: Routledge, 2000.

Kristeva, Julia. *Tales of Love,* tr. Leon S. Roudiez. Columbia: Columbia University Press 1987.

Lechte, John and Maria Margaroni. *Julia Kristeva: Live Theory*. London and New York: Continuum, 2004.

Seager, Ashley. "Record numbers become insolvent as personal debt soars". In *The Guardian*, Saturday 5 May 2007.

Schiffer, James, ed. *Shakespeare's Sonnets: Critical Essays*. New York and London: Garland Publishing, 2000.

Shakespeare, William. *Shakespeare's Sonnets,* ed. by Katherine Duncan-Jones, The Arden Shakespeare. London: Thompson Learning, 1997.

—. *The Norton Shakespeare*, ed. by Stephen Greenblatt, Walter Cohen Jean E. Howard and Katharine Eisaman Maus. New York: Norton, 1997.

Shepherdson, Charles. "Telling Tales of Love: Philosophy, Literature, and Psychoanalysis." In *Diacritics* 30.1 (2000): 89-105.

CHAPTER ELEVEN

COWBOYS AND ROMANS:
CYMBELINE AND PARADIGMATIC CHANGE
IN THE THEATRE

MILES GREGORY

Cymbeline occupies a place in the fringes of the popular Shakespeare canon. It is a play which has resisted attempts at classification and generated a feeling "that its events and the techniques with which they are presented cannot be accounted for in conventional critical terms".[1] The play was written around 1609/10, and first performed in 1610, almost certainly at the Globe Theatre alongside *The Winter's Tale* and *The Tempest*.[2] There is only one extant description of the performance, recorded by Dr. Simon Forman, who apparently saw a production of the play in 1610 or 1611, describing it as "the story of Cymbeline, king of England".[3] The play was first published in the First Folio of 1623. There is a recording of a performance in 1634 at court for Charles I, who is reported to have "well liked" it.[4] After the civil war, however, as is well

---

[1] Warren, ed., *Cymbeline*, p. 10.

[2] We can be fairly precise in our dating of *Cymbeline*: the public theatres had been closed due to plague for most of 1608 and 1609, and for the first half of 1610, during this long interval of closure Shakespeare would have written *Cymbeline*, *The Tempest* and *The Winter's Tale*; parallels in phrasing are evident between *Cymbeline* and Thomas Heywood's *The Golden Age* (1610); and finally, Milford Haven, which features prominently in the play, was fêted in June 1610 as part of the celebrations for the investiture of Henry, Prince of Wales. For a full discussion of the play's probable date see Pitcher, "*Cymbeline* and the Court of King James" in *Cymbeline*, pp. 156 – 157.

[3] Rowse, ed. *The Casebooks of Simon Foreman*, p. 309–311.

[4] See Birch, "Oaths in Shakespeare".

documented, theatrical tastes changed extensively.[5] The "well-liked" *Cymbeline* could no longer be performed without modification: the characters no longer seemed to sit comfortably together in the text; the plot felt increasingly bizarre and improbable; and the language stilted, almost incomprehensible.

Neglected in performance, regarded by academics and practitioners as a play which required major reworking simply to stage, it is therefore potentially surprising that *Cymbeline* has come into its own in the early twenty first century, winning plaudits from theatre reviewers, academics and practitioners. I will argue, however, that there is a simple explanation for this apparently dramatic change in our approach to and reception of the text.

A revolution has clearly occurred in the staging and reception of the play; in fact we have seen a "paradigm shift" in the presentation and reception of the text in performance. Simply put, we moved from a modernist to a postmodernist aesthetic paradigm between 1989 and the early years of the 21st Century, and in performances of *Cymbeline* particularly we can track and analyse the effects of this change.

I wish to consider this performance history of *Cymbeline*, particularly the period 1988 – 2006, through an application of Thomas Kuhn's theory of paradigm change.[6] The parallels between Kuhn's observations on the nature of scientific revolutions and our understanding of the journey between modernist and postmodernist performance of *Cymbeline* are striking.

The principal thrust of Kuhn's work was the identification of "paradigms", which immediately proved an attractive interpretative principle far beyond its own immediate field. His work has been used extensively by academics particularly in sociological, psychoanalytical and philosophical discussions.[7]

Kuhn's approach is similar to that of Dawkins's meme work and the "cultural dominant" of Raymond Williams, and is entirely complementary.[8] Kuhn's theory deepens our understanding of the change in the way *Cymbeline* (and Shakespeare in general) has been performed by

---

[5] For a fuller account see Hume, *The Development of English Drama in the Late Seventeenth Century*.

[6] Kuhn, *The Structure of Scientific Revolutions*.

[7] For further reading on the application of Kuhn's work in disparate fields see Gutting, ed., *Paradigms and Revolutions: Applications and Appraisals of Thomas Kuhn's Philosophy of Science*.

[8] Dawkins, *The Selfish Gene*; also Williams, *Problems in Materialism and Culture: Selected Essays*.

providing a model of the change process which allows for the indeterminacy of cultural change while accounting for the often noted lexical incommensurability between commentators and practitioners working under different paradigms (or cultural dominants). Furthermore, Kuhn's theoretical lens helps us identify the moments when profound cultural change begins; moments which are largely unaccounted for in the writings of Raymond Williams.

The term "paradigm shift" has become a cliché; it is used in everyday conversation to describe a sea-change in our perspective on a particular topic. Prior to the publication of Kuhn's work, the history of science (and indeed knowledge in general) had been generally regarded as linear, progressive and cumulative: that any given cycle essentially built on the work of previous scientists in a gradual and cumulative accretion of stable knowledge.

Kuhn rejected this theory almost entirely. He saw the history of science as one distinguished by periods of intense revolutionary activity, followed by decades - or even centuries - of what he termed "normal science".[9]

The concepts of "normal science" and the "paradigm" are interdependent. Kuhn used the term "paradigm" principally to stand for "the entire constellation of beliefs, values, techniques, and so on shared by the members of a given community".[10] Thus a paradigm serves for a time "implicitly to define the legitimate problems and methods of a research field for succeeding generations of practitioners".[11] The paradigm is reinforced by the teaching process and enshrined in the publication of text books.

"Normal science", or as Kuhn often terms it, "puzzle-solving", forms the research projects and experiments which are conducted under a given paradigm. As Kuhn points out, very few of these experiments carried out in the course of normal science push the boundaries of the paradigm, or indeed are even designed for this purpose. Rather, the purpose of this research is to articulate the paradigm more clearly, to refine ambiguities, to gather factual information pertaining to the effects of the paradigm in practice, and to generally improve the paradigm. Kuhn refers to this kind of research as "puzzle-solving" because like any puzzle the solution must be known before the puzzle can begin to be solved: a jigsaw puzzle would be impossible to complete if the pieces were drawn from two randomly chosen boxes and one was given no picture for guidance. To apply this analogy further we need only think of a paradigm as both the picture and

---

[9] Ibid., p. 10
[10] Kuhn, p. 175.
[11] Ibid., p. 10.

the assurance that all the pieces involved are from the correct set.

Within the history of performed Shakespeare, one can draw many parallels with this process. Shakespeare's own work functions as a textbook for actors, both in the text itself and in performance. Hamlet, famously, gives instruction to the First Player in the practice of acting, advising him "to hold, as "twere the mirror up to nature" (III.ii.22). Indeed, Shakespeare's own theatre saw what might be termed a paradigm shift in the nature of performance, moving away from the two dimensional representations of the morality plays towards a more "natural" style of performance.[12] Within the history of performed Shakespeare we can perceive a succession of paradigms; usually identified by the name given to the predominant style of performance or the historical period in which they occured: "Restoration", for example, or "Realist".[13]

The history of *Cymbeline* in performance generally mirrors that of Shakespearean performance as a whole. From the reopening of the theatres after the English Civil War right through to the late twentieth century, *Cymbeline* rarely enjoyed popularity; during the few occasions when it did attract attention, practitioners have either cut it heavily or rewritten the ending, sometimes both. Thomas D'Urfey rewrote it for the 1682 Drury Lane production as *The Injured Princess; or The Fatal Wager*. William Hawkins, in 1759, found it necessary to heavily rework the play to adhere to neo-classical dramatic unities. David Garrick restored much of the original text at Drury Lane in 1761, but cut three quarters of the final act and removed Posthumus's vision – a vision which was consequently not seen on stage for nearly three hundred years. Charles Macready and Henry Irving, in the nineteenth century, starred as the villain Iachimo in heavily cut and altered productions (usually including large pictorial battle scenes between the Romans and British) which shifted the emotional focus of the play to its heroine, Innogen, who was idealised through the long nineteenth century as, in Algernon Swinburne's words, "the immortal godhead of all womanhood". [14]

---

[12] James Shapiro refers to this shift specifically in a passage regarding Hamlet's quotation from an "old play" to the players – "The rugged Pyrrhus, he whose sable arms,/Black as his purpose, did the night resemble", which Shapiro notes is meant as a kind of nostalgic backwards glance, even as Shakespeare "render[s] the old style of revenge play obsolete". This is consistent, Shapiro further notes, with a "desire to mark the end of one kind of drama and the beginning of another". Shapiro, *1599: A Year in the Life of William Shakespeare*, pp. 323 – 326.

[13] For further reading on a paradigmatic approach to western theatre history, see Gillespie and Cameron, *Western Theatre: Revolution and Revival.*

[14] Swinburne, *A Study of Shakespeare,* p. 162.

Since the late 19th Century, "normal science" productions of *Cymbeline* have sought to resolve the problems of the text (the unevenness, the incoherence, the genre-blurring) by "unifying" the text in performance through an application of the aesthetic tools available in the Modernist aesthetic paradigm.

In 1957 Peter Hall directed *Cymbeline* at Stratford. It was a significant production as it came at a time of great post-war change in British theatre, and it marked the first time since 1761 that the vision of Posthumus had been performed on the stage. The text was cut in parts, but no significant scenes were altered or heavily cut. One of the points on which Hall's production was judged most favourably was that, as T.C. Worsley wrote, he "looked with all the imagination of which he was capable at the play itself to find the principle which will give it unity" and found in it "the point of balance where the pastoral simplicity and courtly intrigue are parts of a logical whole".[15] To do this, Hall created a dreamlike world in which anything seemed possible - the concept allowed the text to "make sense", we might say. The choice to set the play apparently within a fairy tale allowed the disparate and incoherent elements in the text to be absorbed and harmonised. This process was completed by Lila de Nobili's lavish design, complete with grotto and fairy-tale forest.

Modernist unifying strategies were also reflected in William Gaskill's 1962 production in the same theatre, which softened the improbabilities of the plot by using a distancing, storytelling device. The production was set in a rural, quasi-Elizabethan world, complete with jerkin-wearing country folk and fairytale-style wicked stepmothers.

A similar approach was adopted by Barry Kyle and John Barton in 1974, who used a narrator figure to unify the performed text. This function was fulfilled by Cornelius, the Doctor, who maintained a complicit relationship with the audience, stepping outside the action at times to explain and clarify the plot. Attempting to make the play fit contemporary current events, Barton cut over 1,000 lines to emphasise political themes regarding Britain's relationship with Europe.

In 1987/8, for probably the first time in history two major productions of *Cymbeline* were mounted at the same time, both of which attempted to solve the problems of the play by placing it in small, studio spaces, a problem-solving strategy which had produced excellent results with other Shakespearean texts. Bill Alexander in Stratford's Other Place unified the text by following in Gaskill's footsteps and emphasising the storytelling aspects: Alexander placed actors in the audience and highlighted narrative and emotional journeys. It received warmish reviews, but bombed when it

---

[15] Worsley quoted in Warren, *Cymbeline, Shakespeare in Performance,* 35.

transferred to the larger main stage in 1989.

In the Cottesloe at the National in the same year, Hall located the play in a wider structure as part of a season of three late plays; giving theatregoers a production judged warmly by reviewers for uniting the disparate elements of the text through magic and, unsurprisingly given his earlier work on the text, bringing a fairy-tale quality to proceedings.

The directors of these productions, spread over twenty years yet all working under a similar, modernist paradigm, all chose one of two techniques in their attempts to solve the puzzle. They either juggled with the text by cutting or reordering it heavily: the narrator figures, "the storytelling" etc. (Gaskill in 1962, Barton in 1974, and Alexander in 1987/88); or resorted to magic to explain why such strange things might happen (Hall in 1957 and 1988, Jones in 1979).

In a modernist aesthetic paradigm which valued unity through performance, *Cymbeline* was always going to prove problematic. All of these productions can be considered, in Kuhn's terms, as "normal science". The productions in question were puzzle-solving activities; the puzzle was how best to unify through performance the disparateness and incoherence of the text. Reviewers then judged the productions on how well these elements were harmonised; that is to say, on how successfully the problem had been solved. The movement towards a paradigm shift begins with the discovery of anomalous experimental results - results which do not fit in with the picture of reality predicted by the paradigm. The failure of Hall, Barton and Alexander to successfully solve the problem of *Cymbeline*, despite employing all the tools in the Modernist arsenal, was an indication that the current paradigm might be in crisis. Kuhn suggested that "the emergence of new theories is generally preceded by a period of pronounced professional insecurity [...]. Failure of existing rules is the prelude to a search for new ones."

In the fourteen year gap between Barton's production in 1974 and Alexander's in 1988, there had been a gradually renewal of interest in *Cymbeline* in the academic community. The rise of postmodern critical schools such as the New Historicism, Post-Structuralism and later Post-Colonialism provided the academy with new tools with which to approach the text. Alison Thorne, following Derrida, exemplified the post-structuralist approach by celebrating the plays internal linguistic instability; Willy Maley, writing in the new historicist vein, saw the disjointedness of the text as a window into an instable Jacobean imperialism.[16] In drama, too, a new postmodern aesthetic had emerged,

---

[16] Thorne, Alison, "'To write and read/Be henceforth treacherous': *Cymbeline* and the problem of interpretation", p. 176. See also Maley, Will "Postcolonial

although it had not yet penetrated the conservative stronghold of classical performance.

Kuhn posited that paradigm change normally comes in the form of a new piece of major theory which differs in important respects from the previous paradigm, and solves anomalies through innovative changes in technique or approach. Kuhn further predicted that almost always the practitioner who has achieved the fundamental invention of a new paradigm has been either very young or very new to the field whose paradigm they change. As he points out, obviously these are the people who, "[...] being little committed by prior practice to the traditional rules [...], are particularly likely to see that those rules no longer define a playable game and to conceive another set that can replace them."[17]

In 1989 the American director JoAnne Akalaitis read *Cymbeline*. She recalled receiving the play from the Public Theatre in New York. "The first time I read it I said, 'What is this?' [. . .] The second time I read it I saw a whole bunch of things and thought it was very interesting". [18] Her subsequent production of the play would become legendary, and indeed eventually led to the board of the Public Theatre removing her from her post as Artistic Director of the theatre.

Akalaitis, a founder member of Mabou Mimes, had established a reputation for idiosyncratic, irreverent, yet textually faithful stagings of classical texts, which had polarised audiences and critics alike.[19] *Cymbeline* (her first production with the New York Shakespeare Festival – and indeed her first Shakespeare production at all) was to live up to the reputation Akalaitis had forged in the previous decade. As she went into rehearsals, Akalaitis believed she was creating a straightforward staging of the text. In an interview some years later, she claimed that she thought her production would be "very elegant, classical Shakespeare". "We were not," she said, "doing a take on the play [...], a version of the play. [...] We even thought it was rather conservative. We never thought we were doing anything radical." [20]

JoAnne Akalaitis's production of *Cymbeline* opened at the New York Public Theatre on May 23, 1989. Described in a review by Clive Barnes in

---

Shakespeare: British identity formation and *Cymbeline*".

[17] Kuhn, p. 90.

[18] Quoted in an interview with Amy Green, in Green, *The Revisionist Stage: American Directors Reinvent the Classics*, p. 92.

[19] As Green puts it, "a history of controversial, obstinately idiosyncratic restagings" in *The Revisionist Stage: American Directors reinvent the Classics*, p. 91. For more information on Akalaitis's earlier work see Green pp. 90-91.

[20] Quoted in Green, p. 98.

the *New York Post* as a "travesty of Shakespeare",[21] this production would lead to a major and acrimonious critical debate in the New York press and a paradigm change in the way that practitioners and reviewers engage with *Cymbeline*.

Akalaitis described her setting of the play, in a line in the programme, as taking place "In the Midst of Celtic Ruins - A Romantic Fantasy in Victorian England".[22] On stage, the setting was, according to Elinor Fuchs, "One of the most original landscape and environmental settings that has ever been created [...] a miracle of continuous transformation involving turning architectural columns with different scenic faces, backed and enveloped by slide projections of luxuriant vegetation, creeping moss, flinty rocks".[23]

The text was almost completely uncut, and the cast was drawn from an eclectic mix of well known classical actors and those with little previous experience of Shakespeare. Akalaitis had long espoused colour-blind casting, and Cloten was played by African American actor Wendall Pierce; a choice which was ridiculed by reviewers who could not suspend their disbelief at a white queen with a black son.

Many of the reviewers described the feeling of the production as Victorian melodrama meets Elizabethan drama in a highly contemporary modern setting. The production's score was composed by the avowedly postmodern Philip Glass, Akalaitis's ex-husband.

Akalaitis's aim was to use her setting of the play in a Victorian fantasy land to view Shakespeare's original through a notional Victorian "lens".[24] She accordingly came up with a mixture of high melodrama; hints of empire and a nod towards Victorian ideas about history and spectacle. In this, she echoes the play itself, which borrows freely not only in its delineation of character and scene, but also in its time periods and "anachronistic" moments. In a nutshell, Akalaitis never even considered the idea of unifying the play in a consistent setting. If anything, in fact, she *de*unified it, highlighting incoherency and revelling in inconsistency.

The American reviewers responded robustly. John Simon in the *New York Magazine* described the production as "staggeringly, unremittingly, unconscionably absurd [...]. This is a new Shakespearean low [...]: the one direction in which there is no limit is downward".[25] Clive Barnes, in

---

[21] Clive Barnes's review in the *New York Post*, quoted in Fuchs *The Death of Character: Perspectives on Theatre after Modernism*, p. 185.

[22] Quoted in Fuchs, p. 187.

[23] Fuchs, pp. 188 – 189.

[24] Fuchs, p. 187. See also Green, p. 93.

[25] Quoted in Fuchs, p. 186.

the *New York Post* found it a reading "so ignorant as to be effectively below consideration".[26] Referring to the wild swings in the plot, Frank Rich of the *New York Times* asked, "How does a director knit it together? There is no substitute for riding Shakespeare's every dexterous change of mood and style". Rich unfavourably compared Akalaitis's *Cymbeline* with *The Winter's Tale* directed by James Lapine the year before: in his review of that production, Rich admires Lapine for his "ability to knit Shakespeare's many moods into elegant unity".[27] Moira Hodgson, in *The Nation* claimed the music "acts on the brain like a pneumatic drill. [...] it could be the background to an aspirin commercial. Because the play violates the unities of time and space - to put it mildly," she wrote, "unity of style is necessary to bring together the disparate elements."[28]

It all came down to unity of style; judged by the criteria of the dominant Modernist paradigm, Akalaitis's production was a failure. Yet there were many at the time who thought it sensational and superb. The most vocal of these supporters was and is Elinor Fuchs, theatre critic and academic. Fuchs argued that Akalaitis was interested in the idea of "play", using shades of Derridean deconstructive strategies:

> Akalaitis wants play in the system, and does best with texts that invite that play. "Play" means opening up the theatre experience to much more independent signifying status for setting, lights, costumes, and music; it means making a space for actors to bring a range of attitudes to their characters [...]; and it means – just being plain playful. Playful was the casting of the robust Joan Cusack in the leading role of the "divine" Imogen [. . .]. No moment was more irritating to the critics (or enjoyable to the audience) than Akalaitis's most playful one, when Imogen and the faithful servant Pisanio escaped from *Cymbeline*'s court riding a bicycle and a scooter, which silently criss-crossed the stage several times to the accompaniment of a Philip Glass interlude.[29]

History is written by the victors, and in retrospect Akalaitis's *Cymbeline* has been judged as, in the words of Dennis Kennedy, "one of the most remarkable of the new approaches to Shakespeare".[30] Martin Butler, the editor of the 2005 Cambridge edition of *Cymbeline*, regarded Akalaitis's production as an intelligent, original, postmodern approach.

---

[26] Ibid.

[27] Rich, "Fantasy *Cymbeline* Set Long After Shakespeare".

[28] Hodgson, "*Cymbeline*".

[29] Fuchs, pp. 190-191.

[30] Kennedy, *Looking at Shakespeare: A Visual History of Twentieth-Century Performance*, p. 300.

> By filtering an already fractured Renaissance romance through allusions to Victorian stagecraft and its modern appropriations, Akalaitis historicized the meanings accumulated by *Cymbeline* over time, while finding qualities in the play that pre-echoed the rootless post-modernism of her own cultural moment.[31]

How can we be certain, though, that this production truly marked a Kuhnian paradigm shift? Kuhn suggests that the true test of such a change lies in the response by the community in which the practitioner works after a period of reflection on the new techniques and theory. If this new paradigm is accepted by other members of the given community, then a revolution has taken place. The new paradigm becomes a model for practitioners on which to base their work, and a new period of normal science commences.

Just over ten years after Akalaitis redefined the landscape of *Cymbeline* in performance, Brooklyn based Theatre For A New Audience was invited by the Royal Shakespeare Company to be the first American company to perform with them in the UK. Director Bartlett Sher, a renowned Grateful Dead fan, opened his company's interpretation at The Other Place on 19 November 2001. Another production by the RSC was already in the pipleine: directed by Dominic Cooke, it opened at the Swan Theatre on 30 July, 2003.

The two productions, by very different companies and directors, shared a similar postmodern space. In the case of Sher's *Cymbeline*, design and staging highlighted the incongruities of the text, blurring genres to include music-hall style gags, cowboys and samurai. Cooke's *Cymbeline* rehearsed post-colonial interests in a postmodern milieu, focussing more on the relationship between indigenous peoples and imperialistic foreigners. Neither director attempted to unify the text in performance by placing it in a clearly defined period or "naturalistic" setting; neither director made heavy cuts to the text.

The *New York Times*, which had excoriated Akalaitis's *Cymbeline*, had this to say about Sher's:

> Embracing cultural references from Caesar's Rome to medieval Japan to the American West - the centuries-spanning transoceanic duel between a samurai with a sword and a cowboy with a bullwhip is priceless - Mr. Sher's production indulges Shakespeare's gleeful excesses and confusions without sacrificing clarity or accessibility.[32]

---

[31] Butler, ed., *Cymbeline,* p. 67.
[32] Weber, Bruce, "Shakespeare's Grab Bag, Globally Rendered".

Cooke's production was reviewed by the *Daily Telegraph* in equally glowing terms:

> Rae Smith's weird costumes, [are] a curious mix of ancient and modern in which fetishistic furs, feathers and lashings of woad are combined with music-hall bowler hats and regrettable tank tops. It's all a bit of a mess, but so, you could argue, is the play. But Cooke [...] keeps this fantastical show on the road, superbly balancing laughter and tears during the astonishing revelations and reunions in the final act of this fabulously weird and wonderful play.[33]

Almost all reviewers enjoyed the two productions; the *gestalt* had shifted.

It is the weird and wonderful in *Cymbeline*, which for three and a half centuries baffled critics, academics and practitioners, that now acts as a beacon for the post-modern practitioner who sees his or her own life-narrative reflected in the fragmented and decentred world of *Cymbeline*. 1989 saw the birth of the post-modernist aesthetic paradigm in performed Shakespeare. Rather than viewing *Cymbeline* as fractured and incoherent text which required a "solution" to stage successfully, post-modernist practitioners see the unevenness of the text as the very quality they wish to stage. The new paradigm has resulted in a radical rethinking of how, and perhaps even more importantly, why practitioners approach a text. The modernist paradigm of unification has lost its potency; although some practitioners will never adjust to the brave new postmodernist paradigm, we can never return to earlier world views without experiencing them, as it were, in quotation marks.

Appropriately enough, the words of Posthumous Leonatus in V.V.239-243 of *Cymbeline* seem to sum up the relationship between the text and the practitioner today:

> 'Tis still a dream, or else such stuff as madmen
> Tongue, and brain not; either both, or nothing,
> Or senseless speaking, or a speaking such
> As sense cannot untie. Be what it is,
> The action of my life is like it.

---

[33] Spencer, Charles "Even tank tops cannot spoil this fantastical play".

Works Cited

Birch, W. J. "Oaths in Shakespeare". *Notes and Queries*, 6, 8. XII., (3 October 1885).

Butler, Martin, ed. *Cymbeline.* Cambridge: Cambridge University Press, 2005.

Dawkins, Richard. *The Selfish Gene.* Oxford: Oxford University Press, 1976.

Fuchs, Elinor. *The Death of Character: Perspectives on Theatre after Modernism.* Bloomington and Indianapolis: Indiana University Press, 1996.

Green, Amy. *The Revisionist Stage: American Directors reinvent the Classics.* Cambridge & New York: Cambridge University Press, 1994.

Gutting, Gary, ed. *Paradigms and Revolutions: Applications and Appraisals of Thomas Kuhn's Philosophy of Science.* Indiana: University of Notre Dame Press, 1980.

Hodgson, Moira. "*Cymbeline*". *The Nation*, 3 July 1989.

Hume, Robert D. *The Development of English Drama in the Late Seventeenth Century.* Oxford: Clarendon Press, 1976.

Kennedy, Dennis. *Looking at Shakespeare: A Visual History of Twentieth-Century Performance.* Cambridge: Cambridge University Press, 1993.

Kuhn, Thomas S. *The Structure of Scientific Revolutions.* 3rd edn. Chicago: Univ. of Chicago Press, 1996.

Maley, Will "Postcolonial Shakespeare: British identity formation and *Cymbeline*". In *Shakespeare's Late Plays: New Readings*, ed. by Jennifer Richards and James Knowles. Edinburgh: Edinburgh University Press, 1999.

Pitcher, John. "*Cymbeline* and the Court of King James". In *Cymbeline.* London; Penguin, 2005.

Rich, Frank. "Fantasy *Cymbeline* Set Long After Shakespeare". *New York Times*, Thursday 1 June, 1989.

Rowse, A.L, ed. *The Casebooks of Simon Foreman.* London: Picador/Pan, 1976.

Shapiro, James. *1599: A Year in the Life of William Shakespeare.* London: Faber and Faber, 2005.

Spencer, Charles. "Even tank tops cannot spoil this fantastical play". *Daily Telegraph*, 8 August, 2003.

Swinburne, Algernon. *A Study of Shakespeare. The Complete Works of Algernon Charles Swinburne.* Ed. by Sir Edmund Gosse. and Thomas James Wise. Vol. 11. London: Heinemann, 1926.

Thorne, Alison. "'To write and read/Be henceforth treacherous':

Cymbeline and the problem of interpretation". In *Shakespeare's Late Plays: New Readings*, ed. by Jennifer Richards and James Knowles. Edinburgh: Edinburgh University Press, 1999.

Warren, Roger, ed. *Cymbeline.* Oxford: Oxford University Press, 1998.

Warren, Roger. *Cymbeline, Shakespeare in Performance.* Manchester: Manchester University Press, 1989.

Weber, Bruce. "Shakespeare's Grab Bag, Globally Rendered". *New York Times*, 22 January, 2002.

Williams, Raymond. *Problems in Materialism and Culture: Selected Essays.* London and New York: Verso, 1980.

CONTRIBUTORS

Audrey Birkett is in her final year studying for a PhD at Royal Holloway, University of London. Her research focuses on the influences and associations that are reflected in the ancillary material that accompanied the plays of the Caroline era. She has had an essay published entitled 'Henry Glapthorne: Gentleman Poet or Hack Entertainer' in a collection of papers from a previous conference held at Keele University.

Eleanor Collins is completing her PhD on the Repertory of Queen Henrietta's Men at The Shakespeare Institute. She reviews for Cahiers Elisabethain, and has a forthcoming publication on Richard Brome's contract in Early Theatre.

Miles Gregory is a PhD candidate in performed Shakespeare and postmodernism at the University of Bristol. He has worked extensively as a director of Shakespeare and is the director of the Bristol Shakespeare Festival.

Shelly Hsin-Yi Hsieh is a PhD student in the Shakespeare Institute, Department of English, University of Birmingham. Her research focuses on low characters in English Comedy 1576-1603 as well as looks at the lower Stratum of Elizabethan society. The essay in this collection forms part of her thesis, which will be submitted in 2008.

Kristine Johanson is a PhD candidate at the University of St Andrews. Under the supervision of Professor Lorna Hutson, she is currently writing on the rhetoric (particularly *interrogatio*) and politics of Shakespeare's plays of 1595-1605. Her essay '"Only the Mystery": Transforming Fairy Tales & the (Un)Known Self in Timberlake Wertenbaker's *The Ash Girl*" in *International Dramaturgy: Translation and Transformation in The Theatre of Timberlake Wertenbaker* is to be published by P.I.E.-Peter Lang, forthcoming 2008.

Kelly Jones recently completed her doctoral research at the University of Wales, Aberystwyth on the political aspects of self-reflexive theatricality in the plays of Shakespeare and his contemporaries. She now works as a lecturer in Drama at the University of Lincoln.

Michael P Jones read English and Psychology in Liverpool and then travelled the world before returning to academia. He has just completed a double Masters (Renaissance History and the Shakespeare Canon) at the Shakespeare Institute. He wishes to thank the General Editor, Pete Orford, for his clear and calming leadership in both the lighter and darker moments of a project such as this.

Lizz Ketterer is a doctoral student at the Shakespeare Institute, University of Birmingham. Her research interests include early modern English music and song, late Elizabethan and Jacobean dramatic performance, and particularly, the musical practices of the Admiral's Men.

Conny Loder is currently finishing her Ph.D. in English at the Shakespeare Institute, University of Birmingham, UK. Her research focuses on Elizabethan reception of Machiavelli's works. She has published theatre reviews for *Research Opportunities in Renaissance Drama, Cahiers Élisabéthains* and *Penumbra Magazine.* She is a member of the Renaissance Drama Research Group, Shakespeare Institute, Stratford upon Avon. In another life, she was on a Fulbright grant, teaching German at Pacific University, Oregon, USA.

Joshua McEvilla is a third-year doctoral candidate at the Shakespeare Institute. His current research focuses upon post-1630 print culture and the biography of Richard Brome. He is an Assistant Editor of *Future Shakespeares*, Co-general Editor of *The Birmingham Journal of Literature and Language* (a twice-yearly periodical published both electronically and in print), and he was the General Editor of *Perceptions 2003.* He teaches with the third-year Shakespeare module at the University of Birmingham and runs seminars periodically for the same university's literature foundations classes.

Will McKenzie is studying for a PhD in the English and French Departments at Royal Holloway, University of London. His thesis explores the implicit and explicit affinities between Shakespeare, Montaigne and Ovid's Echo-Narcissus story.

Peter Orford completed his PhD at the Shakespeare Institute in 2006, having researched the critical and theatrical background of Shakespeare's history plays in order to explore their potential as individual works of drama, rather than chapters in a cycle. He was a contributing editor to Shakespeare I-learner, an interactive web-based product for school children in Hong Kong, and his article 'The Significance of Venice in *Little Dorrit*' was published in the Dickensian in Summer 2007. He would like to thank the editing team for their valuable input and enthusiasm.

Matteo Pangallo (BA, Bates College; MA, Kings College, University of London) has worked as a research assistant at Shakespeare's Globe Theatre, published in the journal "Notes & Queries", and presented papers at the London Authorship Forum and the American Shakespeare Centre. He is currently a doctoral candidate at the Massachusetts Centre for Renaissance Studies at the University of Massachusetts, Amherst; his fields of interest include textual studies, editorial theory, history of the book, and early modern dramaturgy. At present, he is working on publishing the first modern-spelling edition of *The Launching of the Mary*.

Brian Schneider is a mature (very!) PhD student in the English Department of the University of Manchester. Recipient of a John Bright Fellowship grant in 2003, Brian is now entering his final year of study on the subject of prologues and epilogues in Renaissance Drama - origins and cultural contexts. He is also Administrative Assistant to the five year Lexis project at Manchester, which focuses on both the native and foreign vocabulary of textiles and costume in Medieval England.

Dong-ha Seo is writing a PhD thesis on "Military Culture of Shakespeare's Time" at the Shakespeare Institute. As a member of the Republic of Korea Army, he believes that the investigation of early modern military culture will contribute to understanding of military culture of today.

INDEX